*Here are
ways to make your*

WINDOWS BEAUTIFUL

WHAT'S ONE OF THE MOST PUZZLING PARTS OF HOME DECORATION? IT SEEMS TO BE THE WINDOWS. AND THAT'S THE REASON FOR THIS BOOK. HERE YOU'LL FIND WINDOW "MYS-TERIES" EXPLAINED. YOU'LL LO-CATE SIMPLE ANSWERS TO YOUR QUESTIONS. OF COURSE, THERE'S QUITE A LOT OF OTHER INFORMA-TION THAT WILL HELP THROUGH-OUT YOUR HOME. SO EXAMINE EACH PAGE CAREFULLY. BE SURE YOU GET THE MOST FROM ALL THE GOOD IDEAS YOU WILL FIND.

IFC. (left). It's not just ordinary windows that can be a problem. Handsome double-story ones like these need very special handling. Here, slim panels draw across the vast expanse of glass on less-than-lovely days. Electrac (pages 104, 105) would be a very wise idea.

1

Contents

1-19 Here are ways to make your windows **beautiful.** One of the most puzzling parts of planning any home appears to be the windows — and that's the reason for this book. To explain away their decorating mysteries. This section begins at the beginning. Here, you'll find overall help with home decor, as well as a discussion of things all window treatments have in common. If you, too, begin at the beginning, you'll find each step to your finished window treatments becomes much easier to take.

20-35 Suitable treatments for specific rooms. Is it time to freshen up a room or two? Or are you planning for a brand new home? Either way, you're likely looking for ideas. This section will add to your collection and perhaps remind you of some functional considerations that will guide you in selecting the most appropriate of treatments.

36-51 Suitable dress for the common **window.** It's not a well-known fact, but it is a fact, that no two windows are true twins. Even if they're made to identical dimensions, they can be set into the wall differently. So don't assume anything. Measure everything. But in spite of differences, some specific kinds of windows are more popular than others. This section will help you handle favorite styles.

52-63 Suitable treatments for problem windows. An odd size, an unexpected location, a unique shape. Any of these things can create a problem window. Some unusual windows are truly beautiful. Others are a little shy on charm. But be they focal points or simply ugly ducklings, they all need extra tender loving care if they're to look their very best. This section offers answers to the most frequently found problems.

Hedrich-Blessing, photography.

Decide to be yourself

If there's one decorating certainty these days, it's that individuality is alive and doing very well. But if you're reading this, you have one thing in common with thousands of others just as individual as you. You're interested in your environment.

Environment? Yes. You may live in a city, a suburb or the country, in an apartment, mobile home or mansion, but only you can create your own personal environment. And there's no nicer feeling than honestly enjoying your surroundings.

The best, and most individual, environments are a combination of logic and design. But in planning any project—one room or a home—it's easiest to start by pinning down practicalities. Answer some simple questions up front and you'll establish a direction.

1. Who's going to use the room? Ages and dispositions count. Is it for adults only or will it house toddlers who may scribble on the walls?

2. What will they be doing? Entertaining, sleeping, eating? If peanut butter is going to end up on the floor, the floor should be washable.

3. How will they get from here to there? Set up an easy traffic pattern. It may not stop a teenager from vaulting a sofa, but it will give him a logical alternative.

4. How much can you afford to spend? Be realistic. Can you do some work yourself? Don't overestimate your time, ability or budget.

With these essentials in mind, you're ready for design. Don't worry about the world — it's your environment.

There's nothing wrong with "pure" period furnishings. In fact, they're very

Continued on page 6

4A (far left). Priceless antiques and indoor greenery that anyone can grow. Exquisite velvet draperies on down-to-earth wood poles (page 119). A very "today" print with an oriental rug, an age-old rocking horse. The mixing's done with confidence and color.

5A (above). Some of the nicest dining rooms are done with ladderbacks and tole. Early American warmth is particularly pleasant in this room. Curtains are easy care, simple to sew and protect privacy. Use a curtain rod for the valance, spring pressure rods for curtains (page 122).

5B (left). Nowhere is it written that country living must be in the country. It only takes a scrap of patio and furnishings like these. Sash curtains are well chosen for the look and are also functional at doors. Use sash rods (page 122).

Decide to be yourself

Continued from page 5

Richard Shirk, photography.

lovely. But most people like variety, so instead of tying to "Queen Anne," think formal or informal.

Perhaps you like traditional. It's fairly formal and rich with grace. It offers fine woods, subtle hues, curved lines and dignity.

Casual includes all the "country" styles. Warm and welcoming, its sturdy woods and solid construction take a lot of wear. Textures and earthy colors create a homey atmosphere.

Contemporary and modern are crisp and clean and functional. Color's uninhibited, lines are strong. It's modular, built-in and long on reflective finishes.

Eclectic is the best of all of the above. It hangs an abstract oil above a Victorian sofa. Puts a Shaker table near a Barcelona chair. For best results, let one direction dominate. Use the others as your accents.

Now you have the logic and your look. Do you need a designer or a decorator? Maybe. Maybe not. But do understand they are not one and the same.

A designer is an independent professional, educated to look at the big picture, to know how to assemble an entire package from a variety of sources.

A decorator may be excellent but has less formal training and is usually limited to the products sold by a single store.

If you elect to work with either, communicate! It's essential that they know the

"inside" you if they're to plan your living place.

Do it yourself? Sure. For instance, the rooms in this book are largely the work of highly respected designers, but an idea is an idea. Steal it, scale it down, change it. One leads to another.

What has all this to do with windows? It's prologue. When you begin to turn ideas into real, live rooms, do what professionals do. Begin with the three most important elements. The windows, the walls and the floor. They're most important simply because they're the largest elements in any room. You may find inspiration in a painting or a chair, but if you try to build from small to big, you could lose the major thrust that every good room needs.

So read on. You'll see some of the most beautiful homes in the country. Look at the windows, note how they fulfill the demands of function and design, but don't overlook any ideas that can help you create your own personal environment.

6A (above). If you love things oriental, purity's a plus. This setting hangs together as a piece. But oriental accents can catalyze a host of other moods. Here, sheer draperies draw over the windows and cut-to measure rodding (pages 120, 121) holds a tapestry.

7A (right). Splashes of undiluted color upon big neutral areas are typical of modern. In this bold-line, stripped-down room, a simple window treatment is a must. See-through fabric, in a geometric weave, lets light flow in, but breaks up glare. Draw draperies are on conventional traverse rods (pages 120, 121).

Hedrich-Blessing, photography. Rita St. Clair, design.

Why window treatments?

8A (right). A window with no view can still be beautiful, if you screen out all but light. Here, molding outlines sheer curtains that don't open and side panels that match walls. Both sets of curtains are on spring pressure rods (page 122).

9A (far right top). Keep an eye on kids or enjoy a pretty day through open draperies. At night, when entertaining or in unfriendly weather, cover up the glass. This treatment, hung wide, allows the sliding door to function. A Sherwood traverse rod (pages 110, 111) blends with the paneling.

9B (far right bottom). Privacy and light control combine with good design at two very different windows. A trio of two-way draws over the bed, their closing edges crisply trimmed, become a single unit. One pair does the glass wall. Use conventional traverse rods (pages 120, 121).

Hedrich-Blessing, photography. Adele Keyes and Assoc., design.

A window lets in light and air. Basic, but plan for that function right up front. The beauty comes, in part, from it.

Sun fades and rots some fibers. Where it beats in, a covering can help extend the life of furnishings and carpeting. (Line draperies or use a sun-resistant fabric.)

Another basic. Windows are see-through. The best view can turn ugly when sleet slashes at the glass. Try a part-time covering. Or at a no-view window, use a full-time "screen."

Outsiders may be able to see in. Are you protected from the neighbors and the street? Even with no way to peep, window coverings will make a room more intimate.

Most windows can be opened, and all exchange some inside-outside air. That brings up energy. Conservation's vital and cutting fuel bills, very advantageous.

Consider treatments that let you open windows to a refreshing summer evening breeze. And those which cover up against a white hot sun or chilling winter winds.

Layered treatments provide the most insulation. Use a shade of woven wood with draw sheers and lined draperies and you can still uncover all the glass to open the window.

There's also mental attitude. You won't feel as cold in winter if draperies hide the drifting snow. In summer, a light and airy weave will seem to cool things down.

Work through these practicalities and you'll have an outline for your window treatment. The next few pages will help you fill it out. After that, come dozens of ideas.

Harold Davis, photography. Shirley Freemond, design.

Go on a color kick

Courtesy House and Garden.

There are those who say color is a psychology, a science, an art. And it is all of these. It's also the most fun and the least expensive way to make a new home beautiful or an older home look new.

It's good to know some color facts — not laws. Your personal preference is the one true rule.

All colors come from just three — red, yellow and blue. Add to them their mixes — red, orange, yellow, green, blue and violet. That's the basic color wheel, but the mixes go on endlessly. The true neutrals are black, white and gray, but most soft colors can pass for neutrals.

There are three kinds of color schemes. Monochromatic, variations of one color. Related, side-by-side colors on the wheel, like red, orange and yellow. And complementary, two colors opposite each other on the wheel, for instance, red and green.

Monochromatic schemes are simple and serene. They make small rooms seem larger and can unify a lot of unrelated furnishings. But you've got to love that color.

Related schemes are easy to plan, comfortable, and very popular. They're also open to change as they flow from room to room.

Complementary schemes are dramatic and vibrating. But it takes a lot of know-how to pull them off successfully.

No matter what your scheme, plan it from the large down to the small. First, the walls and floor. Then, windows and the furnishings. Little accents last. Neutrals are the wisest buy for the expensive things. A later change of color is much easier.

Too many colors fragment a room. Use no more than three, but add all the neutrals that you like. And let one color dominate, the others serve as accents. Remember, too, all colors seem stronger in big chunks.

If the room is shy on light, warm it with yellow, red and orange. If it's too bright, blues and greens will cool it down. Warm colors make a room seem smaller and furniture look bigger. Cool ones do just the opposite.

If you're uncertain or just pushed for time, let a designer help. Or "borrow" your color scheme from this or any other magazine. From a poster, a fabric or even a teacup that you love. But bear in mind, it's easier to change a picture than a sofa later on.

Then, check your choice. Gather samples of carpet and fabric, paint, etc. Study them at home in the same proportions that they'll be in the room — a big piece of carpet and smaller swatches of upholstery. Light can alter color and "before" is the time to change your mind.

10A (far left). An exploding blue and toned-down orange complement each other. Whites of sheers and group-defining rug add the color balance. Sheers draw on traverse rods. Slim, trimmed side panels are on cut-to-measure rodding (pages 120, 121).

11A (above left). This tawny monochrome turns hustle-bustle off. Texture's mixed for interest — foil, gilt, velvet, taffeta and a short shag on the floor. A quiet window follows through with cafe-high shirred curtains and side panels on cut-to-measure rodding (pages 120, 121).

11B (above right). High ceiling and brick walls plus all that glass could look clinical, so the related colors used are on the hot side of the color wheel. A casement fabric softens at the window and the simple treatment holds interest in the room. Use a traverse rod (pages 120, 121).

11

Prints charming

Yuichi Idaka, photography. Steve Johnson, design.

Courtesy Window Shade Mfrs. Assoc. Shirley Regendahl, design.

There are devotees of solid colors and fans of multi mixed-up prints. You know which you are, so go with it. But don't rule out a print you like because you're not certain how to use it.

The safe and easy way with pattern is to pick just one and repeat it several places — for instance, on a chair, for pillows and for draperies.

Also safe and easy, choose a pre-coordinated pair of prints. These are special fabrics designed to use together. The bolder one may be a mix of floral and checks. Its coordinate, just checks.

Other patterns, not pre-planned as pairs, are also right for teaming up. If they share their colors, they're likely candidates. If the designs are similar, say both florals, use one big and one small scale print. If the patterns vary, as a geometric and a floral, the scale is much less critical.

A mix of three or more designs is highly individual and harder to do well. All patterns need strong connections of color and of feel.

Now some other tips. Prints get more attention than do solid colors. Too many in a room that's full of furnishings may begin to look like clutter. But if your room is shy on furniture, pattern can minimize the "empty" spots.

Small, allover patterns can wipe out angles you don't like and will visually enlarge a little room. Conversely, big bold prints will make a room look smaller and, used on furnishings, increase size. Dramatic designs used for draperies grow less dramatic. Folds will break them up. But even then, big is still best at larger windows.

Perhaps the most important thing to do before deciding on a pattern is to judge it in your home, in the room where it will live. If you can't get a good sized sample, buy a yard and take it home. If you still like it in a week or two, you'll know that it's a good investment.

12A (left). Lavish is the word, but the pattern message is for everyone. Four can be combined. Walls and windows wear a formal print, as does the border of the rug. But rug diagonals pick up the country-checks of chairs. The French door treatment is on sash rods (page 122), draperies on Kir-Flex rodding (page 123).

13A (above top). Tastefully traditional, this room illustrates judicious use of pattern. Three "unlikes," close in color, grow closer used with well-matched solid shades. Sheers draw on a traverse rod (pages 120, 121), provide privacy while shirred side panels soften the look.

13B (above lower). A team of two done very well. The Pennsylvania Dutch type print dominates through repeated use. An equally informal plaid accents as the curtain lining. Side panels are shirred on a curtain rod (page 122). The cornice could be made at home.

Buymanship

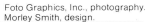

14A (left). Anything's possible when you have it custom-made. Take this one-piece, valance-panel strip that stretches wall to wall, ceiling to floor. It and the undersheers, which draw, are on a valance-traverse rod (pages 120, 121).

15A (above top). Budget buying actually encourages creativity! This zippy, low cost treatment was inspired by the bright wallcovering. No-hem strips of felt repeat its plaid and are simply tacked to two wood poles (page 119).

15B (above lower). Moving and the draperies don't fit? Can't find ready-mades the width you need? Don't despair. If panels are too narrow, as these were, split one and add a solid pair for extra width. Leftover fabric turns into a table skirt. If draperies measure up too short, lengthen with an inset band. Matching undercurtains and a Vintage rod (pages 114, 115) make it seem pre-planned.

Buying window treatments right begins with a list of your priorities and some common sense. To help you sift things out, there's a checklist on pages 136 and 137. Use the facts from it and you're ready to do your shopping.

Now comes a weighty word. "Value." Getting the most for what you pay, regardless of the price. For example, if you sew, you may get the most treatment for the least money. But if you don't have time or patience, it can be poor value.

There's value to be found in ready-made draperies and curtains. Just take them home and hang. The price is pleasing, the fabric and the color choice, quite good. But ready-mades come in limited sizes. They don't fit all windows and they won't go ceiling to the floor. You can get around this, and buy more quality, if you have draper-

ies made for you. Either made-to-measure or custom-made.

With made-to-measure, you provide the store with measurements and select fabric from their samples. The store then orders them from a manufacturer, to your specifications. There are a few limitations and some options. The price is mid-range, depending on the fabric, and there are usually twice-a-year sales. You may want to wait for one.

Custom-mades are just that. The whole beautiful package — wide, wide fabric choice and professional help in the selection. Draperies made specifically for you. Experts measure and install the finished treatment. There are no limitations, and naturally, the cost is higher.

Value applies to more than draperies. It doesn't make sense to hang new treatments on a rod that's seen better days. In fact, new rods may make old draperies look nice enough to keep awhile, and will make inexpensive ones hang better and last longer.

With custom-made draperies, professionals will see you have the rods you need, but there's no secret to choosing them yourself. Stores can offer very good advice. And only the very toughest window problems need hardware that is custom-made.

Just remember, drapery hardware is an area in which you usually get exactly what you pay for. Since it's not a frequent purchase, and very inexpensive in relation to the draperies, it's a good idea to buy the very best.

Fiber in your drapery diet

Foto Graphics, Inc., photography.

Choosing window styles can be such fun that practicality gets swept aside. But if you'll spend just a few minutes thinking "fiber" first, you may save trouble down the road.

Today, all fabrics wear labels. These give their names and fiber content — naturals like cotton and linen, manmades like rayon and nylon. Or blends of two or more. If you know the characteristics of the fibers, you'll know if the fabric's right for you. Labels also list special finishes, to discourage soiling, wrinkles, etc. And there will be care instructions.

What should you look for in a drapery fabric? Obviously, one that drapes well. All of those discussed here do. Test yardage in the store by gathering it into folds.

Then durability. Resistance to abrasion (rubbing) may be a factor if panels touch each other as they draw.

Sun fading. Some fabrics fade more easily than others. With them, use a lining or a sun-resistant undersheer.

Stability. Will a fabric stretch or shrink? Not just when cleaned, but when exposed to varying humidity. Weave can make a difference. Open ones will vary more than closely woven cloth.

Care and flame resistance are important factors, too.

Now, here's a rundown on some of the more popular drapery fibers. Without finishes. Without blending.

Acetate. Acetates have fair durability and resistance to abrasion. They're fair to good at fighting off the sun and quite good for stability. Only fair in resisting fire, some types are washable, others need dry cleaning.

Acrylics and Modacrylics. Fine for durability and both resist abrasion and humidity. Acrylics may darken in the sun, modacrylics won't. Neither will support a flame. Some dry clean, others wash.

Cotton. Very durable, cotton resists abrasion well and is a stable fabric. But it's only fair against sun fading and it will burn. Easy to .wash.

Fiber glass. In all areas, except abrasion, fiber glass gets straight A's for draperies. It's washable, too.

Nylon. Nylon's durable, resists abrasion and humidity. Bright colors can stand sun but softer shades can fade. Nylon melts before it burns. Washable.

Polyester. Polys have the same characteristics as nylon with a bit more resistance to sun fading.

Rayon. Rayon's fair in durability and stability, fair to good in resistance to abrasion and sun fading. But it does burn quickly. Safest care is to dry clean.

Kent Oppenheimer, photography. Mattraw-Vickman Interiors, design.

16A (far left). Lace is a perfect choice for this nostalgic setting. Just keep in mind that open weaves respond to the humidity, so expect some hiking up and down. Shirr curtains superfull on a curtain rod (page 122). Cafes go on a bright brass rod (page 118).

17A (above left). A boy's room must be easy care, but let it be inventive. Here, finish-it-yourself furniture, a painted floor and heaps of a washable fabric work. Bright blue slats hide seams of the car print glued to walls, while a multi-tier cafe stretches the small window. Use Sherwood hand traverse rods (pages 110, 111).

17B (above). Sheer draperies like these come ready-made in many kinds of fabric. White is popular because it doesn't fade (although it can stain) but new processes make color practical, too. Use a traverse rod (pages 120, 121).

Caring for them counts

Sadly, it still happens. A homemaker sends her draperies — which seem to be in perfectly good condition — out to be cleaned. They come back faded or frayed. She blames the cleaners or the manufacturer.

The truth is that the draperies may have deteriorated in her home and the moderate agitation used in cleaning did the damage. Worse yet, neither she nor the cleaners could have predicted it would happen.

Why does it happen? Well, draperies have many enemies. Sun for one. It can cause allover fading or attack a single color. It can create yellow streaks (usually in the glass side folds) that don't show until the dirt is gone. And sun also saps the strength of many fibers.

Fumes from cooking, fireplaces, furnaces, even cars outside, contain chemicals which cling to draperies.

Mixed with humidity and oxygen, they form mild acids which quietly discolor and eat away at fabrics.

Water marks, from condensation on the glass, may hardly show until the draperies are clean. They're almost impossible to remove.

Dyes vary widely. Some clean well, others poorly. Some fabrics stretch, others shrink.

So, to prevent damage, buy your draperies from a reputable store and send them to a reputable cleaner. Buy all the quality you can afford.

Use linings or protective undersheers. The initial cost may be a little more, but you'll save in the long run.

Vacuum brush draperies regularly. Rotate them from sunny to shaded windows every six months if you can. And have them cleaned at least once a year, even if they don't look soiled.

When you send them out, send the care instructions, too. Tell the cleaners what the fiber is. The more information he has, the better job he can do.

Wash only if the care instructions say you can, and exactly as they say you can. If they say hand wash, use the bathtub, never the machine.

If you're thinking about washing "washable" draperies, think twice. Pinch pleats are made with stiffening and, though the drapery fabric may be washable, water may make the pleats go limper than you'd like.

Vincent Lisanti, photography.

Jessie Walker, photography.

18A (above). Drapery damage here could mean redoing the entire room. Be especially aware when using a deep color. It may not show soil, but it's there, and dangerous: A traverse rod (pages 120, 121) controls these attractive panels.

18B (left). Treatments in a child's room should be long-wear and easy-care. Washable curtains are a smart idea. These, on sash rods (page 122), solve an inswinging casement problem.

19A (right). This window may play background to the whammo spread, but it also helps protect it from sun fading. Sheers, like other draperies, last longer with good care. These are on a traverse rod (pages 120, 121).

Leland Lee, photography. Charles Gibelterra, design.

SUITABLE TREATMENTS FOR SPECIFIC ROOMS

TIME TO FRESHEN UP A ROOM OR TWO? OR MAYBE YOU'RE PLANNING FOR A BRAND NEW HOME? EITHER WAY, YOU'RE PROBABLY SCOUTING UP APPROPRIATE IDEAS. AND THE NEXT FEW PAGES WILL ADD TO YOUR COLLECTION. PLEASE PAY PARTICULAR ATTENTION TO THE WINDOW TREATMENTS. HOW YOU DEAL WITH THEM WILL MAKE AN IMPORTANT DIFFERENCE IN ANY HOME, JUST AS THE TWO TREAT-MENTS AT LEFT HELP TO REVI-TALIZE AN OLDER LIVING ROOM.

20A (left). Twin windows in this smallish living room asked for a balance in its furnishings. All is peaceful, yet the pumpkin colors keep it from becoming static. Drapery hardware and other metal accents are in gold. Use Vintage traverse rods (pages 114, 115).

A good-living room

Too often, people who are most creative in their homes don't get off dead center in the living room. They rely on someone else to plan this room, and then they "save" it as a showplace. Do more.

Your living room is the first — and sometimes the only room — that visitors will see. It should tell them instantly just how you like to live. Let it set the tone of your entire home.

Think conversation as you plan this room. Think seating groups, be they plump floor pillows or a formal sofa and side chairs. Think tables, too, for entertaining.

Don't get up tight about the price of "suites." If you can afford just one lovely chair, couch, table, etc., buy it. Add others as you can. That way, you'll have the joy of living with a thing you love.

Traffic patterns are important. Keep home highways clear, especially in the living room. If you don't have an entry, try to make one. It

needn't be a solid wall. It can be a bookcase-room divider. A ceiling to floor panel of a woven wood. Even a sofa back. Just enough to make a break.

In a house, living room windows are apt to face a street. And they'll often be the largest in your home. Since this room is used for entertaining, privacy becomes a major treatment factor. So does sun, because you don't want fading draperies and furnishings.

In an apartment, the floor plan may be reversed and you'll have windows on side walls. The view may be exquisite but frequently, it's just another wall. And that's a case for window coverings.

22A (far left). A rug defines this calm, collected, conversation area. Wide walls of glass would make it all too public so they've draperies for background. Butt two-way draw traverse rods (pages 120, 121) in the corner.

23A (above). Sky-high apartments have built-in privacy, but don't always feel that way. Here, soft sheers and subtle colors keep the interest all inside. Note the self-tied trimmed woven wood valance (pages 124, 125) over draperies on a traverse rod (pages 120, 121).

Housewarming dining rooms

Harold Davis, photography. Elizabeth MacDonald, design.

24A (above). Certainly a mansion, but any home can have the sunny color scheme. And nimble fingers can create a quilted fabric for your chairs. One smashing window wears draperies on a Chateau traverse rod (pages 108, 109) that anyone can own.

24B (right). Cham-pale colors and a wall of mirrors enlarge any too-small area. Up here, privacy's no problem so all-around windows wear an open weave that repeats the textured chairs and breaks up sun as it softens skyline. Use Superfine traverse rods (pages 120, 121).

Morning coffee with a neighbor. Pot luck with drop-in friends. A formal dinner or a simple family supper. Use your dining room. Away from television and confusion, you're free for conversation. And whether you send out for pizza or prepare a show-off meal, it will taste far better in an appetizing room.

It's fine to have matched furnishings in a style that pleases you, but it's by no means essential. A collection of garage-sale chairs can be united with a coat of paint. A battered, but sturdy, table can be fabric-covered to the floor. Build cubes or hang shelving for your serving pieces. Centerpieces? Vegetables and fruit in season. Terry tea towels do double duty as place mats.

Think about color carefully. Most people prefer a quiet background for their food. Purple doesn't do much for digestion. If you stick with semi-neutrals, you can add the accents with your dishes, linens and the like. Easier and less expensive things to change.

Dining room windows vary widely in both size and shape. But it's disquieting to eat your dinner in the street, so make their treatments ones that close. And ones that add charm to the room when closed.

Many dining rooms are open-ended to either living room or kitchen. If this is yours, you'll want to make the floor and walls and window treatments harmonize with those in the related room.

Robert Cleveland, photography. Gary Jon, design.

Courtesy National Homes, Inc.

25A (left). Early Amer-
ican does its warm-and-
welcome thing and cafes
are in keeping. Trimmed
panels on the top are
stressed by a walnut
finished pole (page 119).
The lower tier shields
diners—hangs on a cur-
tain rod. See how sten-
ciling around the mir-
ror makes a "bigger"
piece of it.

Relative to family rooms

Freelance Photographers Guild, photography.

Max Eckert, photography. P. Maas. W. Benner, design.

If you have a family room, you know where to find your family when they're home. In there, watching television, listening to music, playing Monopoly or chess, building bridges out of blocks, reading, studying, popping corn, napping, unwinding, having fun. That's what makes it such a happy room to plan.

Because family rooms do double and triple duty, look for multi-purpose furnishings — those for sitting and sleeping, working and snacking, etc. Turn your live-in carpenter loose to build or to assemble storage space or shelves for hobby things — records, books, games, projectors. Then dress the whole room comfortably and casually.

Choose floor coverings and fabrics for hard wear and easy care. Slipcovers eliminate a lengthy list of house rules and can save a dismal couch or chair.

Paint other castoffs that still function. Nothing has to "go with" anything except in color. And use your favorite colors here — be they way out or down to earth.

Because this is an "open" room, it's nice to let the sunshine in. But because it's just as much a nighttime place, it's also nice to have seclusion. A case for open and shut window treatments.

Woven wood shades and cafes, with or without overdraperies, have a casualness that's right in many family rooms, but there are other ways to go. The fabric you select will do more to set your window's mood than will the treatment style.

26A (top). It's all-American with oriental accents in this tea and conversation room. A slanting window is a problem. Here, panels, hung within the frame to dramatize fabric, are the answer. An easy treatment for a straight-top window, a slant calls for an expert. Use a spring pressure rod (page 122).

26B (lower). A mix of furniture, an offbeat color scheme and fabric shirred on walls exude casual sophistication. Obviously, a "money" room, but you can copy the one color played up with naturals. And "walls," hung on curtain rods (page 122), come down easily to wash.

27A (right). Double-duty, this den turns to bedroom when the sheets show up. And because privacy's essential, there are draperies that draw. Rickrack trimmed, these could be ready-mades or made-at-homes. To help them look their best, hang them on a Chateau traverse rod (pages 108, 109).

A bedroom is for living

Hedrich-Blessing, photography. Ann M. Gray, design.

Harold Davis, photography. Pam Petit, design.

28A (below). Beautiful, big bedrooms have space to unwind, but may need help in looking intimate — especially with a corner full of glass. Here, comfort comes from earth-warm colors and double draw draperies. Use a double two-way draw traverse rod at each window (pages 120, 121).

It's the last thing you see at night and the first when you wake up. Reason enough that this should be a room you love.

A bed is basic — and no place for false economy. Buy the best mattress you can afford. And buy big enough to fit the way you sleep.

There's storage, too. The amount of furniture involved depends upon the closet size, but remember, you don't have to have a "bedroom suite." It's fine to mix the pieces up.

Enough light in the proper places and you've covered the essentials. The rest is up to you. Add a TV. A shelf or more of books. A desk. A place for paints or needlework. Your plants. Your very favorite things.

How you decorate can vary a mile in style. From bedsacks to silk sheets. From lavish spreads to antique quilts. From cool and collected to wildly romantic. From playful to sophisticated.

But no matter how you do what you do, you'll want the windows covered. It's essential for privacy. It's desirable to block too-early morning sun and help save energy. And it's needed for a snug, secluded feeling.

The style and cost of coverings are flexible. A nature person may like shades of woven wood. A romantic will prefer draw draperies on pretty traverse rods that show. A modernist may want to shut the world away with tailored draperies.

So look for ideas, wherever you can find them. Then plan a room that's you.

Courtesy Window Shade Manufacturers Assoc. Shirley Regendahl, design.

29A (top). This room will grow with its young resident— a good idea when you can work it out. Though these are custom, a coordinated throw and window treatment could be made at home. Use sheets, they're tubbable. Draperies, on a Chateau rod (pages 108, 109), are over shades for privacy.

29B (lower). Build in around a window and you've a curl-up reading bench. Pillow slips and draperies began their life as sheets. If you want draperies to draw, use a valance-traverse rod. If not, a double curtain rod (page 122) will do. Privacy comes from a shade like this or one of woven wood.

29

The kitchen...have it your way

30A (below). Natural kitchen ingredients call for equally natural window treatments — woven woods. A Roman *shade lets the windows open and close and its Havasu white pattern (pages 124, 125) ties to sun-kissed colors. Note the* *clever ceiling grid hangs accents high where they don't waste an inch of working space.*

Harold Davis, photography. Tom Quaggin, Tom Hadley, design.

Leland Lee, photography.

Paulus Leeser, photography. Ruth Lynford, design.

31A (left). An open floor plan calls for coexisting treatments. Like this valance over draperies living nicely with a valance plus cafes. Use a valance-traverse rod (pages 120, 121) for one, a curtain and cafe rod for the second. Nice ideas, matching fabric on director's chairs and ceiling beam. Macrame, on a spring tension rod, screens away the living room.

31B (below). An Early American kitchen is always warm and welcoming, even when translated to today. Undersized, stationary side panels let in lots of light and allow the casements to push out. Short wood poles (page 119) wear contrasting rings to pick up the color scheme.

There are all kinds of experts and books and magazines to help you plan a kitchen that runs smoothly. Where the appliances should go, how to arrange the cabinets and the working space. Then it's up to you to make it right for living.

Your cabinets will set the kitchen's mood. If you're not so fond of those you have, and can't invest in new, try paint and fresh knobs and pulls.

Be it tile or carpet, your floor can make a major difference. Install it by yourself and save. Or cover it up with well-anchored scatter rugs.

Kitchen windows often wind up over the sink, wedged between cabinets. Though they may be lackluster now, an inventive treatment can perk up the whole room. Style? Whatever fits your kitchen — from woven woods to something formal if you like. But keep washability in mind.

Think about the view, especially at an over-the-sink window. If it's good, enjoy it with a treatment that just frames the glass. There's not a lot the sun can fade in kitchens. If it's a neighbor's wall or the sun shines in your eyes, a covering will help to keep your spirits high.

Think about function, too. Windows in kitchens are probably opened more often than those in any other room. Let that be a guide.

For accents, use utensils. Even if you're not a master chef, a basket of wooden spoons, a shelf of spices, pans hung in a row, will make you look the part. They're handy when you cook and nice to look at when you carry in.

Bathrooms should be beautiful

Don't divorce your bathroom. If you're unhappy with it, redo it. But remember, it's a member of your family of rooms and it should look that way — like a room, not a "bathroom." Even small ones can.

If you're building or remodeling, you're likely in for some costly fixturing — your builder can offer sound advice, but if you're redecorating, look to little things first. Perhaps you can draw the eye away from your old fixtures. Color's cheap. Imagination's free.

Pinch-pleated fabric shower curtains can hide a less-than-perfect tub. You can even have a shower bar that matches drapery hardware. Screens or folding woven wood partitions make up for missing walls.

Add non-bath, non-custom storage — enameled file cabinets, knock-down shelves. Pretty towels, piled where they'll be seen, may even set a color scheme. Hang things — posters, pictures, bulletin boards. Put out plants. They'll flourish.

And don't neglect the windows. Covering them will give you a comfortable feeling of privacy even if you only overlook the trees. And it will help to cut down drafts. Any treatment is fine, but be selective about fabric. It should be easy care with good resistance to humidity.

Courtesy Imperial Wall Coverings. Abbey Darer, design.

32A (far left). This bandana pattern is a long and lively way from yesterday's more pallid prints. The fixturing is standard. The carpet you could lay yourself. The chest is also do-at-home. And you sew simple curtains. Hang them on a double curtain rod (page 122).

33A (left). Floral paper, framed print and a gilded chair help to make this bath "belong" to the rest of the home. Hung high, pinch-pleated cafes emphasize accents of white and gold (use a bright brass rod, page 118) as they let in natural light, yet still protect privacy.

33B (below). Let the sunshine in through either the top or bottom of this window. The woven wood shade works from the bottom up or from the top down. The wake-up color is lemon mist, the pattern's Carousel and the shade style's double-fold (pages 124, 125).

33

The convertibles...attics and basements.

Hedrich-Blessing, photography. Roberta Lieberman, design.

34A (left). Room to sit and room to sleep in a room that wasn't really a room at all. Floor-length draperies over not-so-special basement walls work their eye magic here. Black and white are foils for other lively colors. Draperies hang from Atavio (pages 112, 113).

35A (right). From grassy green carpet to all aflower walls, this attic garden's fit for a princess. Living greens pick up the well co-ordinated color scheme. Privacy's assured up here so the window only needs to wear a ruffled curtain. Use a double curtain rod (page 122).

In these high-priced living days, every inch of space is valuable, so before you call the movers, check out what you have. Attics and basements can be comfortable. It's what you do, not where, that counts.

Convert your attic to a bedroom. Change a basement to a den that doubles up for guests. These places take imagination, but if they're heat, light and security sound, and you can do the work, they can be fun and economical.

Use just the bare essentials. Rely on dual-purpose furniture. Build in storage where you can. Tuck beds under tables or turn them into seating space when they're not used for sleeping.

Walls may have odd angles. Dark colors and tight, all-over prints will help them fade away. Shirr fabric over badly finished surfaces. Or distract from them with painted butterflies, an array of children's art, bulletin or chalk boards, your hand-hooked rugs or macrame.

Fabrics can be well chosen remnants, denim, pillow ticking burlap. Any of the less expensive types. And you can do the sewing.

For accents, invent. Use baskets, greenery, pillows, fishbowls, bottles, rocks, old umbrella stands or toys.

Windows will be small, if at all. So if you have one, feature it, and be sure you get its light. If you haven't, make one. Frame a mural with draperies. Hang woven wood shades over a blank wall. It's surprising how the eye will fool itself and you won't feel closed in.

SUITABLE DRESS FOR THE COMMON WINDOW

HERE'S A FACT TO REMEMBER WHILE YOU MEASURE. SELDOM ARE THERE TWO WINDOWS EXACTLY IDENTICAL. EVEN IF THEY'RE MADE ALIKE, THEY MAY BE SET INTO THE WALL DIFFERENTLY. HOWEVER, SOME KINDS OF WINDOWS ARE EXTREMELY POPULAR AND SHOW UP FREQUENTLY. AS AN EXAMPLE, THE SINGLE WINDOW PICTURED HERE. THIS SECTION IS FULL OF IDEAS FOR THESE FAVORITE STYLES OF WINDOWS.

36A (left). Common? Only in size. This single window has extraordinary charm. Earth tones flatter mellow woods, as does the rod of gleaming brass. Use a Superfine traverse rod (pages 120, 121) for sunscreening sheers and a Heritage (page 118) for overdraperies.

When your wall is mostly glass

Leland Lee, photography. Tom Williams, design.

A super view begs to be exploited by a wall of glass, but before you decide to leave it bare, try these questions on for attitude.

Do you want to look at that much murk? Or rain? Or snow? Is a sultry summer sun apt to fade your furnishings? Will you really be as private as you'd like in the evenings or when you entertain? Would you like to save on the cost of energy? Then think about some sort of part-time covering.

If the problem's only one of how the weather looks, draw sheers may be enough. For control of sun and inside temperature, and privacy, add draw draperies. Woven woods are fine in either case.

So much for function. As for looks, the window and its view should star. Keep the treatment background simple. You'll find big helpings of a textured weave more interesting than one that's flat and silky smooth. If you're pattern bent, give some thought to tone-on-tone and remember scale. The window's large and chances are the room is too, so choose a sizable design.

Harold Davis, photography. Marilynn Hansen, design.

James Brett, photography.
George van Geldren, design.

39A (top). One window, but it wears two pairs of sheers and also two of draperies. Open, draperies help define the break between the living areas. Closed, they turn it into one warm room. Butt two double Superfine rods (pages 120, 121) close together.

39B (lower left). Nature's colors warm this interior and the woven wood Roman shades (pages 124, 125) see that the sun warms only when and where it's wanted. Using individual shades on individual window sections is a flexible idea that's often possible.

39C (lower right). These comfortable surroundings become even more personal when you're not constantly on view. Draperies, trimmed for the color scheme, draw on an Atavio traverse rod (pages 112, 113).

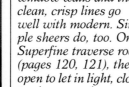

38A (left). Open floor plans often come with window walls and the clean, crisp lines go well with modern. Simple sheers do, too. On Superfine traverse rods (pages 120, 121), they open to let in light, close to give you privacy.

Solutions for doors that slide

John Hartley, photography. Greta Grossman, design.

40A (above). The view's secluded, yet there are times you'll want to close it off. Here, a panel of fabric draws all to one side. The traverse rod is scarcely visible because it's walnut finished to blend with woodwork up above (pages 120, 121).

40B (right). A sliding covering, like this of woven wood, needn't always be at a window or glass door. Use it as a room divider or to screen away a portion of a room. Less costly than building in a sliding door, it gives you texture mixed with color. And should you choose to use woven wood at sliding doors, you'll appreciate its insulation. This pattern's Portola white (pages 124, 125).

Modernage, photography.

Stepping through a sliding door on to a sunny patio can be exhilarating. But that's not true on a cold and rainy day, so why dampen your spirits by looking at bad weather? Some sort of window covering will also help you handle heating and cooling costs and protect your privacy.

Chances are the view outside your door is good and, at times, you'll want all the glass exposed. Do this by having draperies draw back over the wall. A pair can open in the center or a panel pull all to one side. Use the style that works best with your available wall space.

If wall space is at a premium, or the view just isn't inspirational, your draperies can stack back over the fixed glass portion of the door. The other side will still be free to slide.

And hang draperies high enough not to interfere. Put them at least several inches higher than the frame, or on the ceiling's fine.

Sheer or opaque fabric? It's up to you. Evaluate the fading that the sun might do. Lightweight fabrics stack back a little more compactly, but sheers are shy on sun protection.

Print or plain? Again, your choice. Just remember, if you're framing a view, a dramatic fabric will call attention to itself.

41A (right). Apartment cityscapes are sometimes best unseen, though at times you may want to use your balcony. This idea is worth the effort. A glassless frame slides in front of sliding doors. Sheers on sash rods (page 122) fasten to the frame. See how its cross-hatched top echoes the design of tone-on-tone sheers. And how one ferny fabric and the rich mustard color scheme make this room say welcome.

Pretty picture windows

They're called picture windows because they're large enough to frame a view. And they're so popular that builders put them everywhere—overlooking busy streets, the houses next door, etc.

A treatment that covers up the glass at times means that you'll be less exposed. And it will minimize sun damage and help save energy. If the window has sections which open, plan a treatment that can uncover them for ventilation.

So much for practicality. As for dress, you can be far more individual than the standard "uniform" of tied-back draperies and a table lamp.

If the view is one you like, let it be the focal point by sticking to a simple drapery style done in quiet colors. If it's nothing special, play up the window's handsome shape with a more colorful approach that holds attention in the room. Any drapery style (pages 79 to 91) is fine. So are cafes and shades of woven wood. Just harmonize the window with your furnishings — informal with informal and formal with formal.

42A (top). This picture window's dressed for the country-casual room. Crewel-like draperies on wood poles can be hand drawn to block the sun or when entertaining. Cafe curtains add to the informality. Notice how a dark pole (page 119) picks up a color of the drapery while a white one balances cafes.

42B (right). One print in two colors adds to this relaxing room. Shirred fabric adds to warmth and can hide a wall that's worse for wear. On sash rods (page 122), it comes down for cleaning. Curtains over cafes, both on curtain rods, can be released from holdbacks for full privacy. Open-weave woven wood shades just break up the light.

43A (below). A home with picture windows may be traditional outside, but it needn't be inside. Nubby textures spiked with shiny chrome and foil make this room a sleek success. A tiny tone-on-tone stripe in draperies breaks up the view from outside in. They draw on a chrome-like Mod-Rod (pages 116, 117).

Hedrich-Blessing, photography. Alan Portnoy, design.

When you have two or more

Harold Davis, photography. Stanley Avelis, design.

Paulus Leeser, photography. John Maurer, Inc., design.

B efore picture windows, single windows often came in series — one or two or more. That's why they're often found in older homes. Sometimes they'll be standing side by side. Sometimes they're separated by a tiny slice of wall.

As with any window, think first about your need for light and air and privacy. Then hold those functional ideas as you decide which decorating tack to take.

It's possible to treat the span as one nice, wide window. For instance, at a double-wide, use a pair of draw draperies over curtains which will hide the woodwork in between. Or use three fabric panels — a stationary one between a pair. If side panels are on one-way traverse rods, they'll draw to the center one.

If unifying is the way you go, one decorative traverse rod or one valance over all the windows will hold them together.

You can also dress each window in the group individually, but identically. Repetition, even of a very simple treatment, leads to impact. This works well if the windows are a foot or two apart. Then, they'll frame the space between. Use this strip of wall to show off something special — an up-tall set of garden shelves, a macrame wall hanging, bright posters or the like.

44A (top). Triple windows work as one because curtains hide the intervening frames. Panels are made with extra deep top ruffles — put the rod pocket low. A short section of rod pocket and ruffle goes between the panels. To make it even more impressive, the whole is shirred on a Sherwood cafe rod (pages 110, 111). The pretty ends peek out.

44B (lower). A simple treatment gains by being doubled. Notice how gingham outlines all edges of the curtains, just as rich woodwook defines the sunny curtains. Hang them on spring pressure rods (page 122) inside the window frame. If your woodwork's not this nice, paint it a contrasting color.

45A (right). Multi-panels on multi-windows don't draw, but do tie the group together and hide the frames. A wood pole (page 119) stands out against the print to emphasize their oneness. And notice, too, how well the tieback treatment works on the single window in the room.

Paulus Leeser, photography. Bride's Magazine, design.

How to corner well

Don't be intimidated by a corner. It's just like any other window except it has more options.

Do you want sheer curtains? There are curtain rods already bent to turn a corner. Rather have cafes? Use two cafe rods and take off "corner" finials. They slide off without cutting.

Draw draperies? They're done two ways. If you want two panels, one at each window, to close in the corner when you pull one cord, you need a cut-to-measure rod. But if you put a separate traverse rod at each window, you can open and close the draperies independently of one another.

Two adjustable one-way draw traverse rods will look just like the custom version. Use one rod and one panel of drapery at each window.

Two two-way draw traverse rods mean you'll use a pair of draperies for each window and they'll close, not in the corner, but in the middle of the windows. You'll lose a little light if the corner's all glass, but it's a good idea if there's some wall between the windows.

Woven wood shades? Beautiful and easy. Just use one at each window.

A corner window's large and usually quite handsome, so it's best not to get too fussy with its fashions.

46A (left). Cafes hang high for daytime privacy. Draperies close over them when this room is used for sleeping. It's done with two one-way draw traverse rods (pages 120, 121). An easy cornice and an offbeat red-green color scheme are nice ideas to use.

47A (top right). When a corner is a wall instead of glass, try this. Draperies, on two two-way draw traverse rods, make the windows seem continuous. With a combination set (pages 120, 121), you can use draw sheers and draperies plus valances.

47B (top, far right). Glassed-in porches often hand you corner windows. See how well a woven wood fits in. Roman shades (pages 124, 125) raise and lower individually. If you live where seasons change, you'll also like the insulation they provide.

47C (lower right). A spectacular view should be seen most times, but covered up when the occasion's cozy. Draperies on one cut-to-measure or two one-way draw traverse rods (pages 120, 121) are the answer. Steal an idea from this expensive room — draperies that stop short for a ledge won't interfere with baseboard heating.

Those uncommonly beautiful bays and bows

48A (left). This bow combines the beauty of simplicity with the essence of practicality. Fresh yellows seem to make it sunny even when it isn't, and louvered cabinetry hides the heating-cooling system as it forms a spot to show off favorite things. Sheers draw on a cut-to-measure traverse rod (pages 120, 121).

49A (top right). It took a ton of talent to put this room together — now the ideas can be yours. See curves everywhere, beautifully balanced by diagonals of waist-tied curtains and lampshades, and heightened by the sophisticated mix of pattern. Curtains are held, top and bottom, by cut-to-measure curtain rods (page 122).

49B (lower right). This addition, full of windows, is treated as a bay. The wide center span wears two-way draws which close behind the couch. Side draperies pull one-way to the corners. When you've this much glass, individual drapery control is an especially sound idea. Use standard traverse rods (pages 120, 121).

If you've a bay or bow, you've an architectural asset, an instant focal point, an attractive window with sun and view from several sides, and most likely, questions.

First, forget the "can'ts." You can dress these windows almost any way you choose. Some treatments are easier than others. Some take more knowledge, time or money. But almost any style can be done well.

For instance, bows can wear anything except a shade of woven wood. But because each bow is custom-built, its drapery hardware must be custom-made and ordered by your dealer.

Bays, although they come in several shapes (page 69), are easier. If you want one pair of draperies, controlled by one cord to close over the entire bay, you'll need a cut-to-measure rod. But if you treat each window as a unit by itself, you can buy rods right off the shelf. And if you do them one by one, you can have curtains, cafes, any style of drapery and even woven woods.

For instance, use draperies on one-way draw traverse rods for side windows and a two-way draw at the center one. Or use two-way draws on each.

If you've little or no furniture inside the alcove of a bay, use sheers on the window and hang draperies on the flat wall in the room. Closed, they'll simulate a wall of glass.

When tackling a bay or bow, remember it's already handsome. A simple treatment will enhance it. Get complex and you'll upstage it.

Yuichi Idaka, photography. Richard Himmel, design.

Leland Lee, photography. Gaylord Hauser, design.

49

Single windows can be super

Courtesy Imperial Wall Coverings, Collins and Aikman Carpeting. Giorgio Marabito, design.

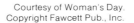

50A (far left). At this recessed single window, the little ledge is used for greenery. Simple sheers form a soft frame for the glass, let the paper and antiques make the major statement. Shirring curtains on a bright brass rod (page 118) is in keeping with the bedstead.

51A (top left). Lots of one romantic floral is the key to this success. And the window gains two ways. First, from the antique brass Chateau rod (pages 108, 109) up above, and next, from the perky ribbon bows which substitute for standard tiebacks.

51B (lower left). An excellent example of how a simple window can help to set a scene. This shades-of-Jefferson swagged valance is perfect for traditional — but difficult to sew at home. It's best to have an expert make it. You'll save on drapery hardware though. It's just a simple curtain rod (page 122).

Single windows? They're those not-big, not-small, ordinary windows some people call "average." But they're not average at all. Those in your home are probably a different size than those in the house next door. So don't shop for a treatment without their measurements.

A single may seem sort of dull compared to other more exotic windows, but it's by far the most responsive. It can wear anything you want it to. Any drapery style, curtains, cafes, woven wood shades — anything.

Budgeting? Singles are a cinch for ready-mades. And they're easy to sew for. In dressy rooms, you may want something custom-made. Likely it's affordable because a single's not that large. That's true of decorative rods, too, which add to its importance.

"Resize" a single window? Sure. With draperies hung wide over the wall. A valance or a cornice on the wall above the glass and frame can up its height a foot or more. Hang curtains or cafes to the floor for an even longer look.

Or be different. Hang draperies on the ceiling and use the wall above the frame for a contrasting paper. Or paint supergraphics all around the window frame. Go formal or frivolous, just so long as that single doesn't come out looking "average."

SUITABLE TREATMENTS FOR PROBLEM WINDOWS

AN ODD SIZE, UN-EXPECTED LOCATION, OR A UNIQUE SHAPE CREATE A PROBLEM WINDOW. SOMETIMES THEY'RE TRULY BEAUTIFUL, LIKE THESE ARCHED FRENCH DOORS. SOMETIMES THEY'RE A LITTLE SHY ON CHARM. BUT LOOKS A-SIDE, THEY ALL NEED LOTS OF TENDER LOVING CARE IF THEY ARE TO FUNCTION WELL. HERE ARE ANSWERS TO FREQUENTLY FOUND PROBLEMS. IF YOUR WIN-DOW IS A VERY DIFFERENT ONE, ASK A DESIGNER FOR HELP IN FINDING PRACTICAL SOLUTIONS.

52A (left). There's double trouble here with arches and French doors. A simple treatment solves both as it adds a light and airy look. Sheer curtains, so easy you could stitch them up yourself, hang on sash rods (page 122) while the lovely, mullioned arches are exposed.

Those puzzling roof-line windows... slanting and clerestory

54A (below). Interesting angles, lots of built-ins and innovative accents are the hallmark of good modern. Clerestory windows add to its geometrics. Here, unlined, single-pleat draperies deliver unexpected light and shadow lines. Hang on Superfine traverse rods (pages 120, 121).

Leland Lee, photography. Ruth Tay, design.

Mobile homes, remodeled homes, brand new homes—cathedral ceilings are everywhere! But what to do with the slanting windows up on top?

Easiest, and usually best, leave the slanted section bare. Treat what's below with draw draperies. They let in light when you want it, block out gloom when it's there and cure that fishbowl feeling.

If sun should be a major problem, you can use a stationary treatment on the slanted glass or over the whole window. But unless you've lots of experience, don't try to make treatments for a slanted window at home. They're really very difficult.

Woven wood shades are good solutions. They can be customized to fit and they raise and lower over all the glass.

A clerestory is another kind of ceiling-high window. Slanted or rectangular, it sits above a wall. Its "plus" is lots of wall space. Its "minus," not a lot of light, so you'll want the little it gives.

The best draperies are simple, made to the window's shape. If you're going contemporary, a bright fabric makes a high-up geometric. If not, match the fabric to the wall to minimize the window's shape. Incidentally, draw cords on a clerestory may be hard to reach, so give some thought to Electrac (pages 104, 105). The switch goes on the wall.

John Hartley, photography. Knowlton Fernald, Jr., design.

55A (top of page). There's not a hint of "assembly line" in this double-wide modular home. It's fresh as well as functional. Even the stationary window treatment is practical. Undo the tiebacks and fabric covers all the glass. Kir-Flex rodding (page 123) holds panels.

55B (above). When you want to bring the outside in, frame it softly with a "quiet" fabric. If the day is less than you'd like, or for privacy, close the draperies. Use a Superfine traverse rod (pages 120, 121) mounted just below the slanted section.

How to arch in triumph

Hedrich-Blessing, photography. Terry Regnier, design.

You may find arched windows in older homes, expensive homes and Spanish architecture. So beautiful but...how?

Begin by vowing that no matter what you do, you won't hide this window's shape. That you'll put all the fabric inside the window frame or put it all outside.

Outside is easiest. Just hang draw draperies on a traverse rod well above the window. Plan the width so open panels frame the window.

Or put draw draperies inside the window frame. The arch goes bare, the rod goes where the sides begin to curve. Do this with sheer curtains, too, if all you need is semi-privacy or sun softening.

Of course, you—or preferably a professional—can also fill the arch. It's fine if you're going formal or restoring an older home and want lovely swags and loopy valances, but think twice before you try it by yourself. They're very hard to sew.

56A (above). Lacy curtains dramatize the window's shape. Here in-swinging casements wear sash rods top and bottom. The custom-made arch covering can be hung on Kir-Flex rodding (page 123).

56B (right). Spicy, Spanish arches wear woven wood. Roman shades. Their bright yarns and tassels are naturals in this environment. They're custom-made to outline arches boldly (pages 124, 125).

56C (far right). And here's a case for understated elegance. Draperies stack well back to let the gentle arch shine through. Although it's obviously an expensive room, the idea's yours to use. The hardware's just a simple traverse rod (pages 120, 121).

Modernage photography.

Leland Lee, photography. Gaylord Hauser, design.

How to right a ranch

Ranch or strip windows, call them what you will, are kissing cousins to clerestories and hand you some of the same problems—not a lot of light and an awkward shape to decorate.

Builders of today's homes put these windows high so you can put furniture below. If you do, stick to a simple window treatment—one that's just apron-long. So that all the light comes in, make draperies wide enough to clear the glass when open. You may want, or have to go, wall-to-wall.

But if you don't put furniture below, you can make a strip look like any nice wide window. If it's very high, cover up part of the top with a valance or a cornice. To make it look longer, hang floor-length cafe curtains at the sill. Only you will know they hide a blank wall.

57A (top). A super answer to a strip! Shutters control the light. A curvy valance and side curtains center attention on the crib. Curved curtain rods (page 122) aren't stocked in every store, but can be ordered for you.

57B (bottom). No picture window here—it's another ranch. The cafe curtains cover only wall. When doing a disguise like this, the draw draperies need be only window frame wide. Draws and cafes are on Sherwood rods (pages 110, 111).

What to do with dormers and small windows

Courtesy Wallcovering Industry Bureau.

Hedrich-Blessing, photography. Bertie Litvin, design.

58A (above). This undersized window went from sad to smashing, helped by a perky paper. Simple curtains, on a simple curtain rod (page 122) pick up a background color and a row of trim coordinates.

58B (right). It's all an optical illusion. This little window's just dressed big. Draperies cover lots of blank wall at each side. A decorative Chateau traverse rod (pages 108, 109) up top, and a pretty band of trim below, reinforce its new-found width.

You'll find dormers only in a gabled roof but a too-small window can show up anywhere. Still, because dormers are usually small, the two have some things in common.

With both, check out the light and air. If other windows give you lots of both, then all you need to do is pick a look you like. If not, then temper taste with function.

If you want a little window to look bigger, it can. Go up on the wall with a valance. Go down with cafe curtains to the floor. Go to the sides with wider-than-you-need draperies. Soon you'll have it looking normal.

Or use a little window to picture frame a fabric that you really like. Or match the fabric to the wall and watch the window disappear. All are valid options.

A dormer, when it's small, hands you a double problem because there's no wall space for disguise. On the other hand, it can become a cozy nook, a space for extra shelves, a tiny, built-in study, even a crib site.

If you're high on dramatics, then you may want to turn the spotlight on with bold and brassy colors, but most people prefer window and walls treated as a single unit. In one color or one pattern. If you need light, keep the colors light and patterns small.

For function, choose draw draperies, cafe curtains or woven wood shades to open as you wish.

59A (left). Dormers can come in double-wides, just right for hide-aways like this. They take more taste than money. The bench seat is an easy project and you sew framing draperies. The wicker needn't be new, just freshly painted. Paint a wood pole (page 119), too, or use a traverse rod (pages 120, 121) wall-to-wall.

59B (below). Tuck your wee one in a dormer. When baby grows, use its extra space for storing toys. This alcove's been defined by paper with a happy trim. Paste more trim along the ceiling line and on a rocking chair. A tiny print's in scale and matching curtains can be made at home. Shirr on a curtain rod (page 122).

A tale of tall and narrows

Long, lean windows used to be a tip-off to an older home, but fashion's come full circle and they're back in popularity. You'll find them used by some of the best architects and builders in the business.

If you love them stretched up tall, keep side panels nice and slim—you can still use draw draperies. Or try woven wood shades that hold the window's shape intact. If the window's inset, and in older homes they often are, shades or sheers can go inside the alcove near the glass, and draperies on the wall outside.

But if you'd rather these windows were rectangular, then make them look that way. Stack back extra fabric on the walls beside. Make them seem shorter with a valance at the top. Use a decorative rod or two—one for draperies, another for contrasting cafe curtains. Add a horizontal trim or pattern, placed-low tiebacks—anything to lead your eye across instead of up and down.

60A (above). Slim and stretching way up tall, these windows fit the architecture of a modern home. Shades of woven wood go with a like design inside. A touch of trim directs the eye up high. Good for privacy and looks, this is Kirsch Surrey white (pages 124, 125).

60B (right). Tall is traditional. This window's been "widened" just a bit with extra fabric on the wall, low-slung tiebacks and a bright brass rod above (page 118). Still it's tall enough to be impressive. If cost is a factor, use sheer curtains, instead of shutters, inside the alcove.

Modernage, photography.

Courtesy Vanguard Studios, Inc.

A case for casements

Jessie Walker, photography. Phyllis Serota, design.

The best news about casements is that newer ones almost always open out. But that doesn't help a bit if you're stuck with older ones that open in.

When your casements crank or push outside, any treatment's practical. But if the open window swings inside the room, make sure your draperies don't tangle in the fabric.

Draw draperies? Fine, if you have them wide enough to uncover all the working portion of the window when they're open. Put draw sheers on traverse rods, too. Or if you're faced with almost steady sun, shirr stationary sheers on sash rods top and bottom. They'll swing open with the window.

Woven wood shades, placed high enough to clear when raised, are super problem solvers. You may want to mount them on the ceiling.

Cafes are out, unless you hang them on the window sill. Then be sure the open window clears the cafe rod and rings.

Valances are possible but, if you opt for them, once again, you'll have to watch the clearance closely.

61B (lower right). These casements could crank in. The ceiling-mounted woven wood shade (pages 124, 125) is high enough to clear the operating portion of the windows. For even more flexibility, an area this wide could be covered by three shades—one for each window—under a single valance.

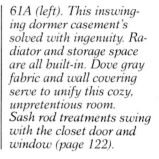

61A (left). This inswinging dormer casement's solved with ingenuity. Radiator and storage space are all built-in. Dove gray fabric and wall covering serve to unify this cozy, unpretentious room. Sash rod treatments swing with the closet door and window (page 122).

John Hartley, photography. Jeannette Coppes, design.

Going door to door

Leland Lee, photography. Mark Nelson, design.

62A (left). Nice and not expensive. Practical, not pretentious. These waist-high sheers let the light come shining through both windows and doors as they provide privacy for seated groups. At doors, they hang on sash rods, top and bottom. At windows, use a single curtain rod (page 122).

63A (top right). One friendly fabric and two friendly kinds of treatments—each doing its own job. Cafe curtains on wood poles (page 119) can be opened or closed as you will. Much of the look-in door glass is covered by curtains, shirred on sash rods top and bottom (page 122). Tiebacks give you look-out space.

63B (lower right). Double French doors may be few and far between, but anyone can treat a single set in this gracious manner. Draw sheers hang high and wide enough to free the door for easy use. Side panels don't draw, just add to the finished look. They're on cut-to-measure rodding (pages 120, 121).

Windows in doors let you look out. Well and good, but windows in doors also let others look in and that may not be exactly what you want these days. So think about them from both sides of the question.

If the window in a front or back door is small, and the view from outside in is limited, you may choose to leave it bare. If the window's half-or-more door size, covering it gives you lots more privacy. Keep the treatment for this kind of window snug. Use rods at top and bottom so the fabric doesn't blow around.

French doors that lead to patios or pretty yards will have a lot more glass (sliding doors are on pages 40, 41). Though you'll want the view at times, there's a case for blocking off your guests' or neighbors' line of sight at others. Treat these as walk-through casement windows, but be sure they're also functional as doors.

At any door, for any treatment, keep the fabric and the "feel" the same as for other windows in the room. That way, they'll all live happily together.

YOU SAY
YOU'D LIKE
WANT TO TO SEW THEM DO YOUR
BUDGET A YOURSELF TREMEN-
DOUS FAVOR, AND STILL HAVE
THE WINDOW TREATMENTS YOU
WANT? SEW YOUR OWN. YOU'LL
WIND UP WITH A REAL FEELING
OF ACCOMPLISHMENT AS WELL.
IT'S NOT THAT DIFFICULT. JUST
TAKE IT SLOW AND EASY, ONE
STEP AT A TIME. BEGIN BY READ-
ING ALL INSTRUCTIONS EVER SO
CAREFULLY. IT'S VITAL TO UNDER-
STAND THEM FIRST. THEN MEAS-
URE EVERYTHING AS ACCURATELY
AS POSSIBLE. AND DON'T WORRY.

64A (left). If you want to sew like a pro, take a long look at their methods. Examine custom-mades in stores, friends' homes, etc. The secret's exacting measurement and careful follow-through. Curtains are an easy way to start. Shirr these on a curtain rod (page 122).

Measuring for rods and treatments

If you have time, patience and can be precise, you'll save money by making your own window treatments. But if you're short on these, it's better to invest in ready-mades or custom-mades rather than take chances.

The instructions on the next few pages are only for basic treatments. If you're ready for more advanced projects, look to your library or sewing and yardage centers.

UP FRONT, YOU SHOULD KNOW THESE THINGS

This is overlap. For privacy, two-way draw draperies overlap in the center of a two-way traverse rod. The overlap is about 2" per panel, so add 4" when figuring the finished width of a pair of draperies.

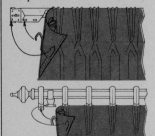

These are returns. A traverse rod projects from the wall so draperies should "return" from the face of the rod to the wall. On a single rod, the drapery return is about 3½" to 4½" but measure to be sure. It will be longer on combination rod sets. Be sure to include returns for both ends when figuring the finished drapery width of a two-way draw treatment.

READ THIS TWICE BEFORE YOU START

Before you begin, assemble all materials and tools — hopefully, someplace where they can remain out until you finish.

You'll need a large, level work surface — a dining room table, several card tables, or as a last resort, a smooth floor. Your ironing board isn't wide enough.

Do all measuring with a yardstick or steel rule. Cloth tapes "give." Keep the fabric flat and smooth but don't stretch it.

If you're a first-timer, start with something easy, like curtains or cafes and work your way up. If it's your first time with draperies, use a solid color fabric and cut out and finish one panel completely before beginning the others. If there should be a mistake, you won't repeat it.

HOW TO FIGURE DRAPERY STACKBACK

With most draw treatments, you'll want draperies to open or "stack back" beyond the window frame and wall to uncover all the glass. To do this, you need to know how much stackback space they will need before you buy the rods or draperies. The chart on this page tells you.

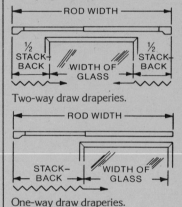

Two-way draw draperies.

One-way draw draperies.

If the glass is	The stackback* should be	Your rod width and drapery coverage should be (Add for overlaps and returns)
38"	26"	64"
44"	28"	72"
50"	30"	80"
56"	32"	88"
62"	34"	96"
68"	36"	104"
75"	37"	112"
81"	39"	120"
87"	41"	128"
94"	42"	136"
100"	44"	144"
106"	46"	152"
112"	48"	160"
119"	49"	168"
125"	51"	176"
131"	53"	184"
137"	55"	192"
144"	56"	200"
150"	58"	208"
156"	60"	216"
162"	62"	224"
169"	63"	232"
175"	65"	240"
181"	67"	248"
187"	69"	256"

Note: Figures are based on average pleating and medium weight fabric. For extra bulky fabrics, add to stackback to compensate for the additional space they require. *For one-way draws, deduct 7" from stackback.

HOW TO MEASURE FOR DRAW DRAPERIES

The rods. Traverse rods should be hung on the wall at the sides of window frame. Put conventional rods 2" above frame, decorative rods 1" above. In either case, rods should be 4" above glass so headings won't show from the outside.

To find rod length, measure width of glass and add drapery stackback, see chart at left. It is best to put rods up before measuring for draperies.

Conventional traverse rod.

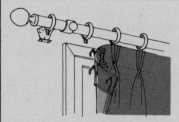

Decorative traverse rod.

The draperies. To find finished drapery width, add 12" (for overlap and two returns) to rod length. For one-way draw draperies, add only 3½".

For finished drapery length, measure from the bottom of decorative rings, or the top of a conventional rod, to the apron or floor. If draperies are to be floor length, subtract 1" for clearance.

HOW TO MEASURE FOR DRAW DRAPERIES OVER DRAW SHEERS

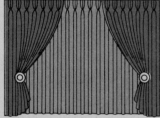

Both under and overdraperies draw.

The rods. Traverse rods should be hung on the wall at the sides of window frame. Put conventional rods 2" above frame, or at least 4" above glass so headings won't show from the outside.

To find rod length, measure width of glass and add drapery stackback; see page 66. It is best to put rods up before measuring for draperies.

Conventional double traverse rod.

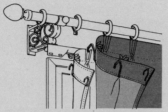

Decorative traverse rod.
Conventional traverse rod.
Double brackets.

The draperies. To find finished overdrapery width, add 18"(for overlap and two 6½" returns)to rod length. For one-way draw draperies, add 6".

For finished overdrapery length, measure from bottom of decorative rings, or top of conventional rod, to apron or floor. If floor length, subtract 1" for clearance.

To find finished underdrapery width, add 4" to rod length. If one-way draw, add nothing. Underdrapery length should be ½" shorter than length of overdraperies.

HOW TO MEASURE FOR DRAW DRAPERIES OVER SHEER CURTAINS

Draperies draw. Curtains do not.

The rods. Traverse rods should be hung on the wall at the sides of window frame. Put conventional rods 2" above frame, decorative rods 1" above. In either case, rods should be 4" above glass so headings won't show from the outside.

To find rod length, measure width of glass and add drapery stackback; see page

66. It is best to put rods up before measuring for draperies. Adjust traverse rod to its maximum projection.

Traverse and curtain rod set.

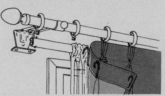

Decorative traverse rod.
Utility curtain rod.

The draperies and curtains. Finished drapery width. If using conventional rod, add 18"(for overlap and two 6½" returns).If using decorative rod, add 14"(for overlap and two 4½" returns).For one-way draw, add 6" for conventional rod, 4" for decorative.

For finished drapery length, measure from bottom of rings, or top of conventional rod, to apron or floor. If floor length, subtract 1".

For curtain width, double or triple width of curtain rod. Curtain length should be ½" shorter than draperies.

HOW TO MEASURE FOR DRAW DRAPERIES OVER CAFE CURTAINS

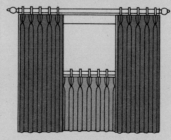

Draperies draw. Cafes can be hand drawn if made in two panels.

The rods. Traverse rods should be hung on the wall

at the sides of window frame. Put conventional rods 2" above frame, decorative rods 1" above. In either case, rods should be 4" above glass so headings won't show from the outside.

To find traverse rod length, measure width of glass and add drapery stackback; see page 66. Cafe rod can be just the length of glass and frame as shown. It is best to put rods up before measuring for draperies. Adjust traverse rod to its maximum projection.

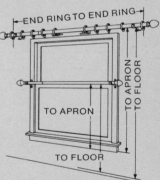

Decorative or conventional traverse rod. Cafe rod and rings.

The draperies and cafes. Finished drapery width. If using conventional rod, add 18"(for overlap and two 6½" returns).If using decorative rod, add 14"(for overlap and two 4½" returns).For one-way draw, add 6" for conventional rod, 4" for decorative.

For finished drapery length, measure from bottom of decorative rings, or top of conventional rod, to apron or floor. If draperies are to be floor length, subtract 1" for clearance.

For finished width of scalloped cafes, double or triple cafe rod length. For pleated cafes, add 6" for two 3" returns. For cafe length, measure from bottom of rings to apron or floor. If cafes are to be floor length, subtract 1½".

Measuring for rods and treatments

HOW TO MEASURE FOR VALANCES OVER DRAPERIES

Valances may be used over single draws, double draws or draw and curtain combinations.

The rods. All types of rod sets should be hung on the wall at the sides of window frame. Put them 2" above frame, or at least 4" above glass so headings won't show from outside.

To find rod length, measure width of glass and add drapery stackback; see page 66. Valance rod will be 2" longer. It is best to put rods up before measuring for draperies.

Valances over single draw draperies

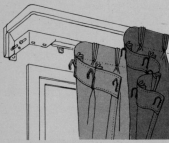

Valance-traverse rod set.

To find finished drapery width, add 12" to traverse rod length(for overlap and two 3½" returns).For length, measure from top of rod to apron or floor. If floor length, subtract 1".

For finished valance width, measure valance rod corner-to-corner; add 14" for two 7" returns. Length is as desired.

Valances over double draw draperies

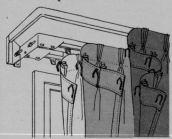

Valance and double traverse rod set.

To find finished overdrapery width, add 18" to traverse rod length(for overlap and two 6½" returns).For length, measure from top of rod to apron or floor. If floor length, subtract 1".

For finished underdrapery width, add 4" to traverse rod length for overlap only. Underdraperies should be ½" shorter than overdraperies.

For finished valance width, measure valance rod corner-to-corner; add 18" for two 9" returns. Length is as desired.

Valances over draw draperies and curtains

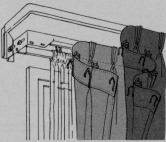

Valance and traverse-curtain rod set.

To find finished drapery width, add 18" to traverse rod length(for overlap and two 6½" returns).For length, measure from top of rod to apron or floor. If floor length, subtract 1".

For finished curtain width, double or triple rod length. Curtains should be ½" shorter than draperies.

For finished valance width, measure valance rod corner-to-corner; add 18" for two 9" returns. Length is as desired.

HOW TO MEASURE FOR CAFE CURTAINS

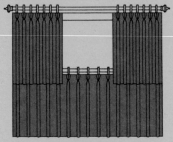

Top tier may be hand drawn. Lower tier can be hand drawn if made in two panels.

The rods. The top cafe rod is usually hung on the wall just above and slightly beyond the edge of the window frame. Adjust it to maximum projection so top curtains will clear lower tier.

The lower rod usually goes on the frame, either centered or about ⅗ of the way up or down the glass.

To find lower rod length, measure width of frame. Top rod should be 2" or 3" longer. It is best to put rods up before measuring for curtains.

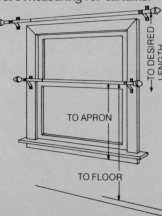

TO DESIRED LENGTH

TO APRON

TO FLOOR

The cafe curtains. For finished width of scalloped cafes, double or triple rod length. For pinch-pleated cafes, add 6" to rod length for two 3" returns.

For length of top tier, measure from top of frame to desired hem. This tier usually covers the second rod and cafe heading, but it may also be made apron or floor length. The second tier may extend to the apron or floor. If floor length, subtract 1" for clearance.

Note: Cafe rings must be purchased separately; they are not included with rods.

HOW TO MEASURE FOR CURTAINS

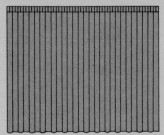

Curtains do not draw.

The rods. Curtain rods are usually hung on the outer corners of the window frame. To find rod length, measure width of window frame.

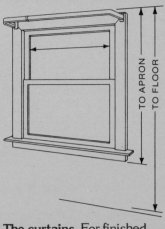

TO APRON

TO FLOOR

The curtains. For finished width of shirred curtains, double or triple rod length.

For length, measure from top of frame to apron or floor. If floor length, subtract 1" for clearance.

HOW TO MEASURE FOR CORNER WINDOWS WITH DRAW DRAPERIES

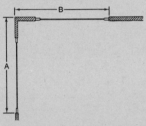

The rods. To find rod lengths, measure A and B and add drapery stackback to each, see page 66. It is best to mount rods before measuring for draperies.

Two one-way draw rods.

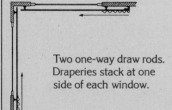

Two one-way draw rods. Draperies stack at one side of each window.

Traverse rods should be hung on the wall at sides of window frame. Put them 2" above frame, or at least 4" above glass so headings won't show from outside. To prevent flaring hems and gapping headings, mount one rod all the way into the corner.

Two two-way draw rods.

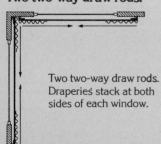

Two two-way draw rods. Draperies stack at both sides of each window.

Position rods as shown for one-way draws unless using a combination rod set — i.e., a traverse-curtain rod. Their extra projection requires that they be butted in the corner.

Two decorative traverse rods

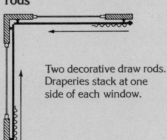

Two decorative draw rods. Draperies stack at one side of each window.

Decorative rods should be hung on the wall at sides of window frame. Put them 1" above frame, or at least 4" above glass so headings won't show from outside. To prevent flaring hems and gapping headings, run one rod all the way into the corner.

Convert decorative rods to one-way draw (instructions in packages). Remove "corner" finials and cut a short section from each rod. Your dealer will tell you how much or do the cutting for you.

The draperies. To find finished drapery length and width, follow instructions on pages 66 and 67 for the type of treatment you desire. For curtains, cafes or special types of treatments, consult your dealer or your designer.

HOW TO MEASURE FOR BAY AND BOW WINDOWS

Two-angle and rectangular bays.

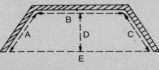

Two-angle bay.

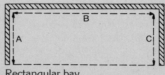

Rectangular bay.

The rods. If windows are to be treated individually, with three separate rods, use measurements A, B and C for rod lengths. It is best to put rods up before measuring for draperies.

Draperies for a bay fit best and hang more gracefully on cut-to-measure rods. For estimating costs of custom rod and draperies, take all measurements shown, but have your dealer or designer remeasure before ordering.

The draperies. If using three separate rods, find finished drapery width and length by following instructions on pages 66 and 67, depending on the type of treatment you desire. If treatment is to be custom-made, your dealer or designer will measure for you.

Four-angle bays and bow.

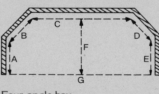

Four-angle bay.

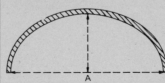

Bow window.

The rods. No two four-angle bays or bow windows are identical so all drapery hardware for these types of windows must be cut-to-measure. For estimating costs, take all measurements but have your dealer or designer remeasure before ordering.

The draperies. It is best to have draperies for these windows custom-made. Your dealer or designer will measure for you.

HOW TO MEASURE FOR WOVEN WOOD ROMAN SHADES

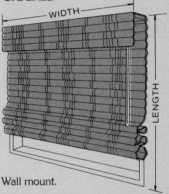

Wall mount.

Wall (outside) mount. Measure width and length of window including frame. To prevent light gap, add a minimum of 3" to both measurements. Tell your dealer you want an outside mount and if cords should be on right or left. Select valance style desired.

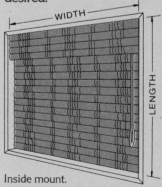

Inside mount.

Inside (recessed) mount. Measure width and length inside window frame. Measure width at top, center and bottom; shade will be made to clear narrowest width. Tell your dealer you want an inside mount and if cords should be on right or left. Select valance style desired.

Making your window treatments

Shirred curtains. Cafe curtains. Shirring fabric on walls.

SHIRRED CURTAINS

1. Measure. To find your finished curtain measurements, see page 68.

To measure for your fabric, double or triple the width of your curtain rod. Add 4" to each panel to allow for double 1" side hems. Add 6" to desired length to allow for a double 3" bottom hem. Add another 3" for a top hem.

If your fabric is a print, allow for pattern matching. See page 76.

2. Cut out. Cut off selvage, or if fabric ravels easily, clip selvage at ¼" intervals.

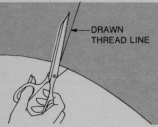

Panels must be cut straight. If the weave is loose, pull a thread from the fabric and cut along the "line" it leaves. If the weave is tight, chalk a line along a yardstick.

3. If you need to join widths of fabric. Put the pieces to be joined on top of each other, right sides together. Extend the bottom piece ¼" beyond the edge of the top piece.

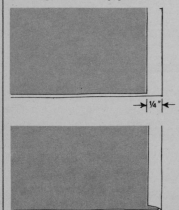

Fold extended edge of the bottom piece over the top one and press.

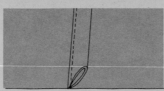

Make a second slim fold, this time with both pieces of fabric. Pin and press. Sew by hand or on a machine set for 8 stitches to the inch.

4. Make double 1" side hems. Fold fabric in 1" and press. Fold over again, press and pin a few inches at a time. Sew with long, loose stitches.

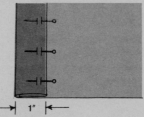

5. Make double 3" bottom hem. Fold fabric up 3". Keep bottom edge on same thread across the entire width. Press. Fold up another 3". Press, pin and sew.

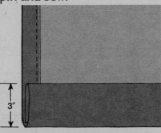

6. Make top hem. Fold fabric down 3". Press. Fold raw edge under ¼". Pin and sew with long, loose stitches.

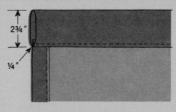

7. Make rod pocket. Seam across the top above the top hem. Pin and "try on" rod before sewing. Allow about ½" clearance for easy shirring. Back stitch ends.

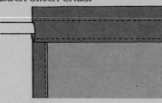

CAFE CURTAINS

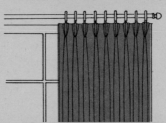

Pinch-pleated cafes. These are made like pinch-pleated draperies except there are no center overlaps.

See page 68 to find finished cafe curtain measurements. See pages 72, 73 for sewing instructions.

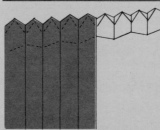

Accordion-pleated cafes. These are made with Kirsch Wonderfold, a self-pleating buckram.

See page 68 to find finished cafe curtain measurements. To find fabric meas-urement, double the finished width and allow for side and bottom hems. Also allow 3½" for top hem. Hem sides and bottom of panel. Make 3½" top hem and insert Wonderfold. Hang with clip-on rings.

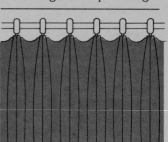

Scalloped cafes. See page 68 to find finished cafe curtain measurements. Use medium to heavy fabric. Scallops in the tops of a sheer fabric may droop.

1. Make a paper pattern. These instructions are for a 48" panel. Adapt them to your required width.

Cut a sheet of paper 48" wide and draw a straight line across the top. Fold to find center.

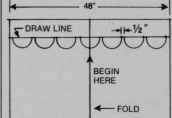

Use a saucer or other round object about 6" in diameter and draw half circles from center to outer edges. Leave ½" points between scallops. If you don't come out even, adjust width of outer points. Remember to allow for side hems.

2. Put in hems. Hem sides and bottom of panel. Lay right side up and fold down the depth of scallops plus 2" for top hem.

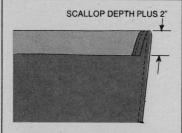

SCALLOP DEPTH PLUS 2"

3. Make scallops. Center cutout pattern on panel with points on fold. Trace. Stitch along this line. Cut out scallops leaving ¼" of fabric outside of stitching. Clip this ¼" every inch or so to prevent puckering.

4. Make top hem. Turn heading right side out and press. Turn raw edge under and pin or paste. Stitch in hem.

5. Hang. Use clip-on rings for each fabric point or use eyelet rings with drapery hooks.

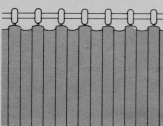

Tubular cafes. See page 68 to find finished cafe curtain measurements. Use this style only where panels will be stationary. Tubular pleats do not open and close well.

---

1. Make a paper pattern. These instructions are for a 48" panel. Adapt them to your required width.

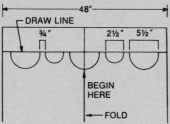

DRAW LINE ¾" 2½" 5½"
BEGIN HERE
FOLD

Cut paper 48" wide and draw a straight line across the top. Fold to find center.

Center and draw a 5½" diameter scallop on this fold. Alternate 5½" scallops with 2½" scallops, working toward the edges. Leave ¾" points between scallops. If you don't come out even, adjust width of outer points. Remember to allow for side hems.

2. Put in hems. Hem sides and bottom of panel. Lay right side up and fold down the depth of scallops plus 2" for top hem.

3. Make scallops. Center cutout pattern on panel with points on fold. Trace. Stitch along this line. Cut out scallops leaving ¼" of fabric outside of stitching. Clip this

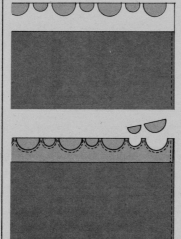

¼" every inch or so to prevent puckering.

4. Make top hem. Turn heading right side out and press. Turn raw edges under and pin or baste. Stitch in hem.

5. Hang. To hang, roll small scallops into tubes, lapping one point over the next. Secure tubes with clip-on rings.

CAFE RINGS

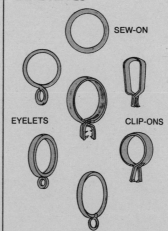

SEW-ON
EYELETS
CLIP-ONS

There are three types. Eyelets — used when you hang curtains with drapery hooks. Sew-ons — sewn to the curtains; remove them for laundering. And clip-ons — these have prongs which grip the fabric.

You must buy rings separately. You'll need three for every foot of rod. Add one if your cafes are made as a single panel. Add two if they are made as a pair.

SHIRRED FABRIC WALLS

Shirred fabric on walls is more than handsome. It can hide uneven or cracked surfaces and disguise minor flaws. It is easily removed for cleaning. Use lightweight opaque fabric. Sheets are suitable. For an example, see photo 42B.

1. Measure. To find finished area, measure width and height of wall. To measure for fabric, double the wall width. Add 4" for double 1" side hems. (If using hemmed sheets, omit this allowance.) Add 6" to desired length for 3" top and bottom hems.

If your fabric is a print, allow for pattern matching (see page 76).

2. Mount rods. Use cut-to-measure oval rodding or curtain rods with close projection. Because they'll bear a lot of weight, do not extend them full length. It is essential to fasten brackets to wall studs. Place them about 1½" down from ceiling and up from floor.

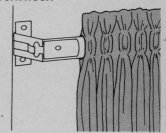

3. Hem sides and top. Follow instructions for side hems and rod pocket as shown for curtains, page 70.

4. Hem bottom. Hang fabric on top rod. Pin in bottom hem, compensating for irregularities in height. Remove and make rod pocket as you did at top. Shirr fabric on both rods.

Making your window treatments
Unlined draperies. Simple top treatments.

UNLINED DRAPERIES

Choose your fabric. Try to avoid delicate types that sun fade easily and, unless making draw sheers, avoid loose weaves that should be lined for body. If you're a beginner, it's also best to avoid loose weaves.

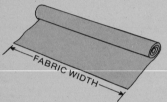

"Fabric width" refers to the width of the fabric as it comes from the bolt. To obtain desired drapery fullness, you may have to seam two or more fabric widths together. You can join full widths or half and quarter widths.

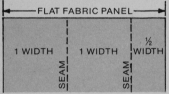

"Flat fabric" refers to the seamed panel before the pleats are put in.

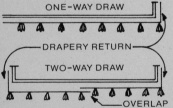

This flat fabric must be pleated down to obtain your desired drapery coverage.

If using a two-way draw traverse rod, make two panels for each window, each panel half of the desired coverage. If using a one-way draw traverse rod, make just one panel.

1. Measuring. To find your finished drapery measure-

ments, see pages 66 to 69.

To find your flat fabric size, locate your desired panel coverage in column 1 of the chart below. This is pleated coverage for one panel, not total coverage. You will need two panels for two-way draw draperies.

Column 2 gives you the flat fabric width required. It's all right if you're off a little. You can adjust later.

The flat fabric measurements are for treatments on a single traverse rod. If using a double rod set, add 3" to the outer edges of the panels for the longer drapery returns required.

Find flat fabric length by adding 16" to your finished drapery length. This is for double 4" top and bottom hems.

Multiply this length by the number of fabric widths you need to get the total yardage for one panel. Do this for each panel you are making.

If your fabric is a print, plaid or stripe, you must allow extra for pattern matching. Your store can figure this or see how to do it on page 76.

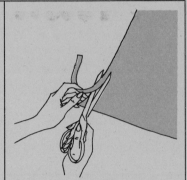

2. Cutting out. Cut selvage off fabric or if fabric ravels easily, clip selvage at 1" intervals. If you need to join two widths together, follow step 3 on page 70.

1 Desired Pleated Panel Coverage	2 Flat Fabric Without Hems	3 Hemmed Flat Fabric	4 Number of 4" Flat Spaces Between Pleats	5 Number of Pleats	6 Width of Fabric in Each Pleat
16"	43"	39"	4	5	3⅛"
20"	51"	47"	5	6	3¼"
24"	59"	55"	6	7	3⅜"
28"	67"	63"	7	8	3½"
32"	75"	71"	8	9	3½"
36"	83"	79"	9	10	3⁹⁄₁₆"
40"	91"	87"	10	11	3⅝"
44"	99"	95"	11	12	3⅝"
48"	107"	103"	12	13	3⅝"
52"	115"	111"	13	14	3⅝"
56"	123"	119"	14	15	3¾"
60"	131"	127"	15	16	3¾"
64"	139"	135"	16	17	3¾"
68"	147"	143"	17	18	3¾"
72"	155"	151"	18	19	3¾"
76"	163"	159"	19	20	3¾"
80"	171"	167"	20	21	3¾"
84"	179"	175"	21	22	3¾"
88"	187"	183"	22	23	3¾"
92"	195"	191"	23	24	3¾"
96"	203"	199"	24	25	3¾"
100"	211"	207"	25	26	3¾"
104"	219"	215"	26	27	3¾"
108"	227"	223"	27	28	3¾"
112"	235"	231"	28	29	3¾"
116"	243"	239"	29	30	3¾"
120"	251"	247"	30	31	3⅞"
124"	259"	254"	31	32	3⅞"
128"	267"	263"	32	33	3⅞"

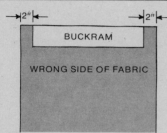

3. Make heading. For most draperies, use 4" buckram. Cut a strip 4" shorter than the width of the flat fabric panel. (Buckram will not extend into side hem folds.) Center buckram on wrong side of panel even with the top edge. Pin, then baste in place. Fold fabric down 4". Fold down again, another 4". Pin bottom edge.

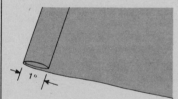

4. Put in side hems. Fold fabric in 1" and press. Fold over another 1", press and pin or baste. Machine or hand hem with long, loose stitches.

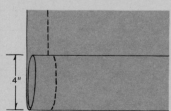

5. Put in bottom hem. Recheck desired finished length. Panel should now be 8" longer than this measurement. If it is, make 4" double bottom hem. If length varies, make adjustment in depth of hem. Fold fabric up 4", press. Fold over another 4", press and pin or baste. You may want to cut out excess fabric where it folds over side hems. Machine or hand hem with long, loose stitches.

6. Make pleats. Find your desired pleated panel coverage in column 1. If your hemmed flat panel is the same width as that in column 3, use the number of 4" spaces and pleats shown. Column 6 gives you the amount of fabric to be used to make each pleat.

If the width of your hemmed flat panel differs from that in column 3, adjust like this. Add 7" (10" if using a double rod set) to your pleated panel coverage (column 1). Subtract this from the actual width of your hemmed flat panel. Divide this by the number of pleats in column 5. The result is the amount of fabric in each pleat. Use the number of flat spaces shown in column 4.

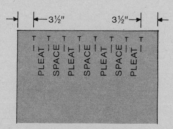

Pin pleats and flat spaces. Begin 3½" in from side of panel — 3½" is the return for a single rod. If using a double rod set, begin 6½" in. Pleats will end 3½" from opposite edge of panel. If making a pair of draperies for a double rod set, remember the longer return is needed at the outer side of each panel.

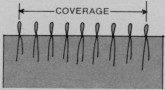

Pin sides of pleats together and remeasure coverage. If needed, let out or take in pleats slightly.

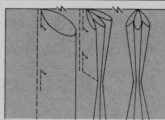

Stitch pleats where pinned, top to bottom of buckram. Make three small pleats of the one large fold. Tack front to back at bottom of triple pleat grouping. Finger press firmly to crease buckram into pleats.

HOW TO MAKE SIMPLE TOP TREATMENTS
Leave complex, swagged top treatments to professionals who do them best. Here are a few that anyone can do.

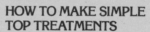

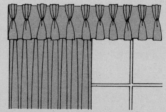

Pinch-pleated. Make like a short pinch-pleated drapery. Hang on valance or cafe rod.

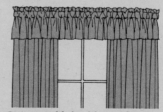

Shirred. Make like a short shirred curtain.

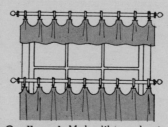

Scalloped. Make like a short scalloped cafe curtain.

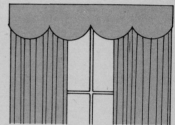

Flat and shaped. Make a paper pattern. Cut fabric and hem sides and bottom. Make a rod pocket at the top.

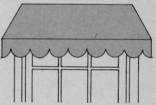

Canopy. Make paper pattern. Cut out, hem sides and bottom. Make pocket for curtain rod at top and canopy rod near lower edge.

Cornice. Make paper pattern. Add 2" to rod projection and 2" to rod length for drapery clearance. Add 1" for side hems. Fold to find center.

Fold fabric double, right sides in. If a print, center design. Trace pattern. Hem bottom and sides. Cut out, leaving ¼" of fabric outside stitching. Clip curves. Turn right side out, press.

Make cornice of ¾" board. Depth should stop short of design. Put up drapery hardware, then mount board with angle irons.

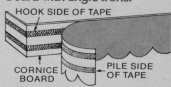

Attach fabric to board with Velcro pressure sensitive tape.

73

Making your window treatments

Lined draperies. Using pleating tape. Shirring over poles.

LINED DRAPERIES

Choose your fabrics. The lining and drapery fabric must be compatible in terms of wear and care. If you have questions about which fabrics are compatible, your store can help you with selection.

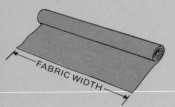

"Fabric width" refers to the width of the fabric as it comes from the bolt. To obtain desired drapery fullness, you may have to seam two or more fabric widths together. You can join full widths or half and quarter widths. You may also have to join lining widths together.

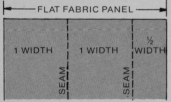

"Flat fabric" refers to the seamed panel before the pleats are put in.

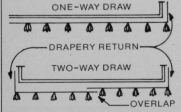

This flat fabric must be pleated down to obtain your desired drapery coverage.

If using a two-way draw traverse rod, make two panels for each window, each panel half of the desired coverage. If using a one-way draw traverse rod, make just one panel.

1. Measuring. To find your finished drapery measurements, see pages 66 to 69.

To find your drapery flat fabric size, locate your desired panel coverage in column 1 of the chart on page 72. This is pleated coverage for one panel, not total coverage. You will need two panels for two-way draw draperies.

Column 2 gives you the flat fabric width required. It's all right if you're off a little. You can adjust later.

The flat fabric measurements are for treatments on a single traverse rod. If using a double rod set, add 3" to the outer edges of the panels for the longer drapery returns required.

Find flat fabric length by adding 8½" to your finished drapery length. This is for double 4" bottom hem and ½" top turn-under.

Multiply this length by the number of fabric widths you need to get the total yardage for one drapery panel. Do this for each panel you are making.

If your fabric is a print, plaid or stripe, you must allow extra for pattern matching. Your store can figure this or see how to do it on page 76.

The flat fabric needed for a lining will be 5" narrower and 7" shorter than that of the drapery panel.

2. Cutting out. Cut selvage off drapery fabric or if fabric ravels easily, clip selvage at 1" intervals. If you need to join two widths together, follow step 3 on page 70.

Pink selvage of lining fabric. If you need to join two widths, use a simple single seam.

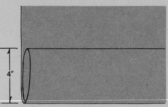

3. Put in bottom hems. Fold drapery fabric up 4", press. Fold over another 4", press and pin or baste. If using weights, sew them to wrong side of fabric in the corners. Machine or hand hem with long, loose stitches.

Make a 2" single bottom hem in lining panel, turning raw edge under.

4. Attach lining. Lay hemmed lining panel on top of hemmed drapery panel, right sides of both fabrics together. Line up at top and right edge. Smooth, pin or baste down the side, ½" from edge. Sew.

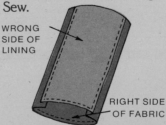

WRONG SIDE OF LINING

RIGHT SIDE OF FABRIC

Slide lining over to left hand side of drapery panel so that raw edges of both panels are even. Pin or baste down this side, ½" in from edge. Sew.

Because the lining fabric is narrower than the drapery fabric, the panel will bell out.

Pink raw edges of both panels, on both sides, to prevent raveling.

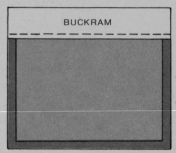

BUCKRAM

5. Make heading. Center the lining panel on the drapery panel. Smooth.

Cut a strip of 4" buckram to the panel width. Pin this strip to the panel so that the bottom edge of the buckram overlaps the top edges of the drapery and lining panels by ½". Stitch across the bottom edge of the buckram.

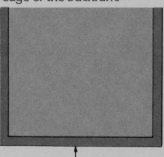

OPEN AT BOTTOM

Drapery and lining panels are now joined at the top and both sides. They are open at the bottom. Buckram extends from the top.

Turn this "pillowcase" right side out, concealing the buckram. Panel is ready to pleat.

6. Pleat panel. Pleating a lined panel is done in the same manner as pleating an unlined panel. Follow the instructions given in step 6 on page 73.

MAKE DRAPERIES THE EASY WAY WITH EASYPLEAT® HEADING TAPE AND HOOKS

Easypleat is a pre-shrunk, stitched-pocket heading tape that automatically spaces and forms pleats when you insert Easypleat hooks in pockets. You sew only straight seams.

Regular Easypleat produces draperies of double fullness. Double pocket Easypleat has twice as many pockets for more flexibility and fuller pleats. Either may be used for lined or unlined draperies.

UNLINED DRAPERIES

1. Measuring. Find flat fabric width as if you were making regular unlined draperies. See step 1, page 72.

To find flat fabric length, add 8½" to your finished drapery length. This is for a double 4" bottom hem and ½" top turn-under.

To figure width of tape, add 1" to each hemmed flat panel width. To be sure you have enough, buy an extra half yard.

2. Cutting out. Cut panels following step 2 on page 72.

3. Put in side hems. Side hem following instructions in step 4 on page 72.

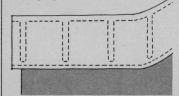

4. Make heading. Turn panel right side up and lay tape across top raw edge. Cover ¼" of fabric at the top and overhang tape ½" at each side. Pocket openings must point up. Pin or baste tape to fabric. Stitch.

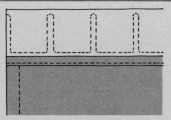

Turn the drapery panel over. Fold Easypleat tape back so that it lays across the wrong side of fabric. Fold side overhangs under the tape and sew. Stitch along the bottom of the tape making sure to sew below the pockets.

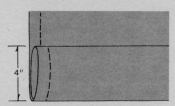

5. Put in bottom hem. Recheck your desired finished length. The panel should now be 8" longer than this measurement. If it is, proceed to make a 4" double bottom hem. If the length varies, make an adjustment in the depth of the hem.

Fold fabric up 4", press. Fold over another 4", press and pin or baste. You may want to cut out excess fabric where it folds over side hems. Machine or hand hem with long, loose stitches.

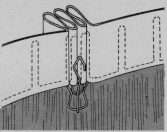

6. Pleat panel. Insert one prong of hook in each of four pockets. Skip three pockets and repeat. Use pin-on hooks at master slides and for returns.

LINED DRAPERIES

1. Measuring. Find flat fabric widths and lengths for drapery and lining as if you were making regular lined draperies. See page 74.

To figure width of tape, add 1" to each hemmed flat fabric width for draperies. Do not use lining width. To be sure you have enough tape, buy an extra half yard.

2. Cutting out. Cut panels following step 2 on page 74.

3. Put in bottom hems. Hem, following instructions in step 3 on page 74.

4. Attach lining. Follow instructions in step 4, page 74.

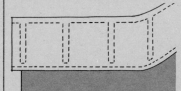

5. Make heading. Turn panel right side out. Lay tape across top of drapery fabric side. Cover ¼" of fabric at top and overhang tape ½" at each side. Pocket openings must point up. Pin or baste. Stitch.

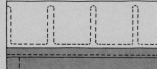

Turn the drapery panel over. Fold Easypleat tape back so that it lays across the wrong side of fabric. Fold side overhangs under the tape and sew. Stitch along the bottom of the tape making sure to sew below the pockets.

6. Pleat panel. Insert one prong of hook in each of four pockets. Skip three pockets and repeat. Use pin-on hooks at master slides and for returns. See illustration column 2 this page.

SHIRRING FABRIC OVER WOOD POLES OR CAFE RODS

One of today's popular looks is to shirr curtains over wood poles or cafe rods. Round poles and rods add an interesting dimension to headings and finials protrude from rod pockets for extra beauty.

However, this type of treatment is best done at windows under 48" wide with light to medium weight fabric. Longer rods require supports and shirred headings will not slip over supports. This means you must slit headings in a wide panel or use several panels at a wide window.

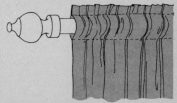

Find finished measurements as for shirred curtains; see page 68. Find fabric width as for shirred curtains; see page 70.

If using a 1⅜" diameter wood pole, add 6⅝" to desired curtain length. Make double 3" bottom hem and 2½" top hem. If you wish a ruffle above the rod pocket, add 1" for this.

If using a 1" diameter cafe rod, add 6⅜" to desired curtain length. Make double 3" bottom hem and 2" rod pocket. If you wish a ruffle above the rod pocket, add 1" for this. Cafe rods come in varying diameters, so be sure to check this measurement carefully.

Proceed to make curtains following instructions on page 70, altering only the size of the rod pocket. Shirr over rod or pole before attaching finials.

Making your window treatments

HOW TO MATCH PATTERN

 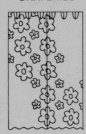

FLAT PANEL   DRAPERIES

SEAM

When making draperies, the pattern on flat seamed panels must match. Pairs of panels must match when the draperies are closed. And all panels in a room should match.

The best and easiest way to be sure you have enough fabric to match pattern is to have the store figure it for you, based on your finished drapery measurements and the repeat of the fabric you choose, but you can do it yourself.

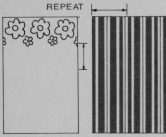

REPEAT

Pattern repeat. A repeat is the lengthwise measurement of one motif, or the crosswise measurement of a set of uneven stripes. A solid color may also have a texture pattern, like a slub thread which is repeated at regular intervals.

You will need one extra repeat for each length of fabric you will be using. You may need an extra width if dealing with stripes. Remember, if you are seaming fabric widths together, get an extra repeat for each width. Before cutting, decide where you want the pattern to fall.

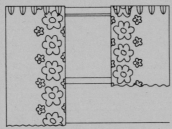

Ideally, there would be a full repeat at the heading and another at the hem, but this isn't always possible.

If it's not and you are making floor-length draperies, use a full repeat at the heading and a partial one at the hem. If you are making apron-length draperies, use a full repeat at the hem and a partial one at the heading.

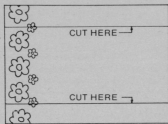

CUT HERE

CUT HERE

Next, cut one panel to position the pattern as you desire.

To do this, you will need to cut off a total of one repeat—but you'll cut some from the top and some from the bottom—not all from one end and no more than one pattern repeat in all.

You now have a "master" panel. Match each of your other panels to this by lining them up and marking the selvage before you cut.

HANGING AND TRAINING YOUR DRAPERIES

How you hang your draperies does make a difference in the way they look and operate.

Begin by putting a drapery hook, at the proper height, in each pleat and at back of returns. Always use pin-on hooks at master slides and for returns.

Begin to hang panels at the master slide. Attach hook in each successive ring or slide. Do not skip rings or slides — instead, push extras to the end of the rod.

CONVENTIONAL TRAVERSE ROD

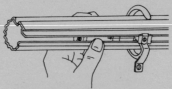

DECORATIVE TRAVERSE ROD

Remove leftover rings or slides through the end gate on the rod. (Should you need to add more rings or slides, slip them through the end gate now.) If extra rings or slides are left to hang free between those which are used, they may twist and interfere with the smooth operation of the rod.

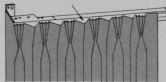

CONVENTIONAL TRAVERSE ROD

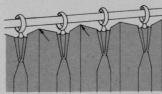

DECORATIVE TRAVERSE ROD

All drapery headings, your made-at-homes or custom-made, new or newly cleaned, must be trained to "fold up" gracefully when the draperies are opened. You teach them by "breaking" the headings.

If you are using a conventional traverse rod, place

your finger behind a flat space between pleats. Firmly hand press to break the heading forward. Repeat this across the entire panel. If headings are allowed to break at random or turn toward the rod, they can drag along its face and make operation difficult.

If you are using a decorative traverse rod, break the heading in the same way, but push it back toward the window. The heading rides below the rod and can't interfere with its operation.

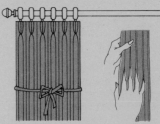

When the draperies have been hung and the headings have been broken, open them up fully. Form professional looking folds by firmly finger pressing each fold down a foot or two.

Tie folds loosely in position using cotton tape or heavy twine. Continue pressing and tying every foot or so to the bottom of the panel. Leave the panels tied for two or three days while the fabric develops a memory.

After a few days, untie the draperies. For the next few days, open and close them regularly to shake out any remaining wrinkles.

Some ins and outs of traverse rods

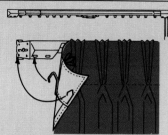

Conventional traverse rods. This type of rod opens and closes draperies when you pull a cord. It can be adjusted in length and in the distance it projects from the wall. Thus, it fits windows of varying widths and draperies made with varying returns. When closed, draperies cover conventional traverse rods.

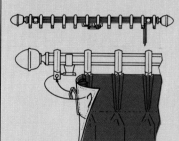

Decorative traverse rods. This type of rod is also cord operated and adjustable in length and the distance it projects from the wall. Draperies ride below a decorative traverse so the rod is seen at all times.

Half-round ring slides. The rings on a decorative traverse rod are open in the back, allowing them to slip over rod supports. They do not touch the surface of the rod and cannot mar its finish. Rings on cafe rods and wood poles are full round and hang directly from the rod or pole.

Rod diameters. Decorative traverse rods are available in 1" and 1⅜" diameters. While the look of the larger rod is usually preferred, the 1" version is in scale with narrow windows and is suitable for use with lightweight draperies.

Cafe rods come in many diameters. Again, proportion is a primary consideration.

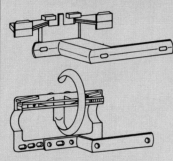

Master slides. Masters are the slides with arms. They are the only slides attached to the cord and they pull the leading edges of drapery panels. There are two in the center of a two-way draw traverse rod and one on a one-way draw.

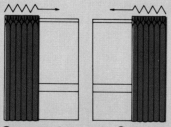

One-way draw rods. One-way rods are either right-to-left or left-to-right. To determine which you need, stand in front and look at the window. Do you want the draperies to be on your right hand side when they are open? Then, you want a right-to-left hand draw. If you want the fabric to be on the left, you need a left-to-right hand draw.

Decorative rods do not come in one-way draw, but

they can be "converted." Each Kirsch package contains easy to follow instructions, or ask your store to do this for you.

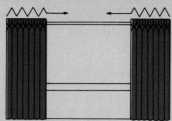

Two-way draw. This type of rod closes a pair of draperies in the center of the window.

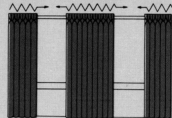

Multiple draw. This type of treatment takes a custom-made rod. With it, several drapery panels are controlled by one rod.

Combination rod sets. This term refers to any combination of two or more rods. Most two-rod combinations are pre-packaged for you — for instance, double traverse and double curtain rods. Some three-rod sets, involving a valance rod, are not. You buy the double rod you want and a separate valance rod kit. Easy instructions are in the valance package.

Doubling up with decoratives. Decorative rods don't come packaged in double sets, but combinations are easy to do.

If using a decorative with a conventional traverse or another decorative, get the double brackets designed to hold both rods. They automatically align the drapery headings.

If putting a decorative over curtains, use a Series 3700 utility curtain rod. They come with parts for combination.

Support spacing. Supports are packed with longer rods. If there is only one support, center it in the middle of the rod. If there are more, space them to be where the fabric weight is heaviest when the draperies are open.

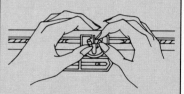

If draperies don't draw. This almost never happens, but if it should, it's more than likely that the cord has become unhooked. It should be tucked under the tab on the back of the master slide. If it has slipped out, open the draperies and tuck it back under.

Check the left master first. It's usually the culprit.

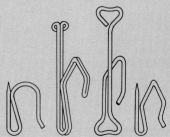

Hook selection. The proper hooks can make or break a drapery treatment. They help headings stand erect and aid in a smooth drawing operation. There are many kinds, but you'll find the proper ones listed on the package of the traverse rod you buy.

WHAT THE WELL-DRESSED WINDOW WEARS TODAY

DOES IT APPEAR THERE'S NO END TO THE FETCHING WAYS A WINDOW MAY BE DRESSED? WELL, TO SOME EXTENT, THAT'S TRUE WHEN YOU CONSIDER ALL THE HANDSOME FABRICS AVAILABLE TODAY. BUT IT'S BEST, AND EASIEST, IF YOU PICK THE TYPE OF TREATMENT YOU WANT FIRST, BE IT RATHER FORMAL, AS AT LEFT, OR SOMETHING MUCH MORE CASUAL. THE NEXT FEW PAGES WILL EXPLAIN THE LATEST WINDOW FASHIONS.

78A (left). Mix spoon-smooth cafe au lait and cream with silky textured fabric and you have traditional that's absolutely elegant. The window treatment is the same. This valance is the type that professionals do best, but the sheers and double curtain rod are easy.

Basic draw draperies

Measuring instructions on pages 66 and 67

Leland Lee, photography. Andrew Gerhard, design.

If you want all-way control of sun, light, air and privacy, you're thinking draw draperies — pinch-pleated panels on a traverse rod, opened and closed when you pull a cord. The simplest of these puts one layer of fabric between you and the glass.

There are three basic kinds. Most popular is the two-way draw — two panels which close in the middle of the window.

Next up is the one-way draw, useful at corner windows, bays and sliding doors. One panel pulls all from one side across the width of the entire window.

On a right-to-left hand one-way rod, the open drapery will stack back on the right as you face the window. On a left-to-right hand one-way, the fabric will pile up on the left.

A third kind is multiple draw — several panels, all controlled by one rod. Most useful at vast walls of glass, this special treatment takes a cut-to-measure rod.

Traverse rods are "conventional" or "decorative." A conventional rod is covered when the draperies are closed. A decorative rod stays in sight regardless because draperies ride below it.

You can put traverse rods on the ceiling. On the wall — the recommended place because open draperies will uncover all the glass. On the window frame if you must. Or on the ceiling of a recessed window area.

Any fabric which contributes to the room is suitable. Think seriously about linings if sunlight is a factor.

Robert Cleveland, photography.
Saddleback Interiors, design.

80A (top left). In love with daring color? Use it, but add balance with some quiet areas. Here, draperies provide the "resting place." These are on a conventional traverse rod in a walnut finish (pages 120, 121). It fades into the window frame when draperies are open.

80B (bottom left). Even when you don't intend to draw your draperies, but close them by undoing tiebacks, it's best to use a traverse rod. These rods are designed to help hold pleats erect. Here, view-framing panels are on a ceiling-mounted conventional rod (pages 120, 121).

81A (right). A semi-opaque, textured fabric creates a cozy conversation mood, yet doesn't block out all the light. Open draperies to invite the view inside. This well-shaped window is subtly defined with a Chateau traverse rod (pages 108, 109) up top and bands of woven-in-the-fabric trim below.

Hedrich-Blessing, photography. Bertie Litvin, design.

For extra flexibility, double draw draperies
Measuring information on page 67

Jessie Walker, photography.

Richard K. Shirk, photography.

Harold Davis, photography. Barbara Jewel, design.

Put two layers of fabric between you and the glass, both cord-drawn, and you have one of the most flexible of treatments — double draw draperies.

On a nice day, open both and the window if you like. For semi-privacy, or to screen back sun, close the glass-side set. To save air you've warmed or cooled, or for total privacy, close both.

You can use double draws in pairs. Two pairs of pinch-pleated draperies, both closing in the center of the window, take a double two-way draw traverse rod set. Or use two wide panels, each pulling from one side across the entire glass. Each takes a one-way traverse rod.

Rods are conventional or decorative. The conventional kind won't show when draperies are closed. They're sold as sets, two rods with double brackets.

Or use a conventional rod for underdraperies and a decorative rod room-side. Or use two decoratives. But when there's a decorative rod involved, do buy special brackets offered separately. Because they hold both rods and align both drapery headings automatically, they're worth their weight in ease and beauty.

Double draperies can be hung from the ceiling, on the wall, or on the window frame if wall space is super critical.

Usually the underdrapery is a sheer or open weave, the overdrapery opaque. But two sheers can be a smashing combination, too.

82A (far left). This comfortable room is a masterpiece of mix-manship, from modern art to antique ink wells. The traditional fabric strikes a middle-ground. At the window, sun-filtering draw sheers with privacy-protecting overdraperies, plus valance. Use a triple rod combination set (pages 120, 121).

83A (top left). Quiet tailoring suits this modern dining nook. Sheers let you breakfast in the sun, overdraperies let you dine in privacy. Use two one-way draw conventional traverse rods (pages 120, 121).

83B (above). Formal, yet wise use of warm woods and color keeps the room from being "cold." See how the weave of underdraperies reflects the patterned chairs. A fabric like this, made with extra fullness, breaks up light and view so well that overdraperies can be tied back on most occasions. Use a double traverse rod (pages 120, 121).

John Hartley, photography. Harry Gladstone, design.

Another "flexible"...
draperies over shades of woven wood

Measuring information on pages 66, 67 and 69

84A (left). While this custom shade of woven wood (pages 124, 125) provides all the function needed at this wall of glass, the room gains grace and elegance from the added draperies. These, on cut-to-measure rodding, don't draw, but they could, if you use a ceiling-mounted traverse rod (pages 120, 121).

85A (right). One pattern welds twin windows and the entire room together. A sill-long shade of woven wood (pages 124, 125) sidesteps the touchy radiator situation as it provides total privacy. Use a wood pole (page 119) or a decorative traverse rod and a pair of draperies to reinforce the idea of a single, nice wide window.

Courtesy, Good Housekeeping. Ann Heller, design.

There's a really neat, new look in window fashion and it's super functional as well. Team draperies with shades of woven wood.

Now, on pages 96 and 97, you'll see there's a ton of flexibility to woven woods when used alone — control of light and air and privacy — but there are other places where adding draperies makes even better sense.

For instance, if your window needs the soft look of framing fabric panels.

Or if you're out to solve a radiator problem. Use shades to the sill, floor-length draperies at both sides, away from the heat source.

Or when you want the maximum in insulation. Two coverings — one of woven wood, the other of lined draperies — are about the very best around.

Or when you want to muffle noise, say from a very busy street, the two make perfect partners.

The easiest way to do this double-up treatment is to mount the shade inside the window frame and put draperies on the wall, just as you would a single pair. And it's almost as easy to hang both from the ceiling.

As for patterns, there are woven woods to form a quiet background, others to coordinate with draperies and still others to create color-texture interest of their own to use with solid color fabrics.

85

Draw draperies go over curtains, too

Measuring information on page 67

Let's start with definitions. Pinch-pleated draperies, hung on traverse rods, draw to open and to close. But because curtains slip over a rod, they're stationary. So while there's not a lot of difference in the appearance of draw draperies over draw sheers and that of draw sheers over curtains, there's quite a bit of difference in the way each type of treatment works.

In both cases, the draperies draw to help you conquer light and give you privacy. And like draw sheers, curtains do filter sun and screen the view. But keep in mind, they're always between you and the glass. In their favor, they can be inexpensive to buy and easy to make. The choice is yours.

The traverse rods you'll use can be one or two-way draw — the draperies and the curtains made in one wide panel or in pairs. The traverse rod style, conventional or decorative.

If you opt for a conventional traverse rod, use a combination set that holds the traverse and the curtain rod on one pair of brackets. With a decorative traverse, use a utility curtain rod beneath.

The treatment can go near the ceiling — it takes an inch or so to shirr on the curtain. On the wall is good, because open draperies will clear the window area. Or they can go on the frame if absolutely necessary.

Normally, curtains are sheer or an open weave, but if the view's unsightly or the sun is bright and steady, they can be opaque.

86A (far left). When the need for privacy prevails, reverse the "normal" order of the fabrics. Put opaque curtains under sheers that draw. The rod which does so much for French Provincial furniture is a Chateau traverse (pages 108, 109).

87A (above). A money-saving tip when you want a viewless window to look wider. Buy or make your curtains just window-frame wide. Hang draperies, with valance if you like, wider on the wall. Use a curtain rod plus a combination valance-traverse rod set (pages 120, 121).

87B (right). When draw draperies are hung like this, the eye can't tell if there are curtains or draw sheers beneath. Made full, the curtains look lavish. Here, they're on a utility curtain rod, while draperies hang on a Sherwood traverse rod (pages 110, 111). Holdbacks come with extra long arms so they can be mounted on the window frame.

Couple cafe curtains with draw draperies

Measuring information on page 67

Is "casual" your theme? You'll like this look. Or are you slightly formal? Makes little difference. Fabrics key this treatment's mood.

As for function, this team has a lot. Through open draperies, you'll have light and sky, yet still retain your seated privacy. Make cafes in pairs that open and you can bare the total glass. Close draperies for full privacy or extra "insulation."

How much glass goes bare depends on where you put the cafe rod. It's best somewhere off dead center. Put it higher for more privacy, lower if you need the light. Even put it on the sill to make a too-short window look floor length.

Usually cafes are wed to two-way draw draperies, which close in the middle of the window. But they can marry one-way draws at corner or bay windows, if each window is treated as a separate unit.

There's double impact when you use matching cafe and decorative traverse rods. Or use your favorite cafe rod with a conventional traverse rod above.

Mix or match your fabrics, too. A sprightly print for cafes, a solid for draperies. Or patterned draperies with a plain cafe. Or both alike.

When cafes are used with draw draperies, it's best to pinch pleat headings of the cafes, too. That rule can bend, but identical headings are never, never wrong.

Jessie Walker, photography. Shirley Lynn, design.

88A (left). There's no room for furniture inside this shallow bay, so the treatment's done with that in mind. Cafes and shades are for privacy. Draperies on the flat wall close for a cozy mood when tiebacks are undone. Each window section wears a cafe rod with finials removed. They and the decorative traverse rod are Chateau (pages 108, 109).

89A (above top). The setting's traditional; the valance, formal; and the cafe curtains, beautiful. The low "wall" of fabric holds interest in the room, makes the skyscrape background. Draw draperies and valance are on a combination valance-traverse rod set (pages 120, 121), while cafes hang from a bright brass rod (page 118).

89B (above lower). Color it sunny and you're halfway to happy family dining. But this mood-setting window also solves a problem. It unites twin windows. Draperies, seldom drawn, hide the window frames. Cafes, hung from almost-sill to floor, help to complete the illusion. Sherwood traverse and cafe rods (pages 110, 111) stress togetherness.

89

Tip-top treatments

Measuring information on page 68

Courtesy, National Homes

op treatments have few things in common, so let's start with the two they have. First, they're strictly for appearance. Second, many are not do-it-yourself. They may look easy, but they demand professional know-how.

Now for variables. A top treatment may be used just because you like its looks. Or to solve a problem — to unite several close-together windows, to cover part of one that seems too tall, to add inches over one that looks too short.

You may use a cornice or a valance. A cornice is wood — polished and carved, painted, or fabric covered.

A valance is fabric — swagged, ruffled, flat or pleated in a host of ways. Ruffled and pinch-pleated ones are safe to sew at home. So are some made-flat styles. But if there's swag or draping to the one you like, seriously consider having it custom-made.

A cornice board is hung with angle irons and covers up the drapery hardware (see page 73).

Heavy, complex valances also hang from boards. Less complicated ones use rods. A combination valance-traverse rod set will hold a simple style and draperies. You'll need to add a separate valance rod to double rod sets.

If you want eye action up on top, but the cornice-valance route seems expensive or confusing, try a decorative traverse rod instead. It's a pleasing "extra," and less costly than a custom treatment.

Leland Lee, photography. Harvey Ackerman, design.

Hedrich-Blessing, photography. Adele Keyes and Associates, design.

90A (far left top). Ruffled valances can be sewn at home. If the hem is straight, make them like a mini-curtain. If curved, try an inexpensive fabric first to be sure the curve falls where you want it to. Use a valance-traverse rod set (pages 120, 121).

90B (far left bottom). Unpressed box pleats form a valance that is soft, semi-formal and not too difficult to make. Designing is the hardest part. Try out the width of pleats and spaces in between with paper or scrap fabric first. Here, a valance rod's used with a double traverse set (pages 120, 121).

91A (left). There are a thousand versions of this swagged valance and all are beautiful. But few should be home-sewn. The gracious draping may look simple and straightforward, but it takes an expert to accomplish. The hardware's easy though. Use a valance-traverse rod set (pages 120, 121).

Cafe curtains and their kissing cousins

Measuring information on page 68

Yuichi Idaka, photography. Guy-Hayden Assoc., design.

These days, it's pretty hard to classify a cafe curtain. The scalloped styles which hang from rings on cafe rods — no question, they're cafes. Others are pinch-pleated. That really makes them shorty draperies, but on a cafe rod they're transformed to cafes. Then there are shirred curtains, hung mid-window, where a cafe rod would go. Close, but they don't qualify because the rod's a no-show style.

It used to be that cafes were always two short tiers. Not now. You'll see them hung in three or more. Or as one tier, plus or minus valance. Or as floor-length panels. Or almost any other way.

Why so popular? Because the look is comfortable and, obviously, versatile. Also many versions let the window function fully.

Make cafes as pairs, instead of in one panel, and you can cover or uncover glass at will. Control the light and air and your degree of privacy. But remember, cafes are hand-drawn — no cord — so be sure the fabric's easy care.

Choosing cafe rods is half the fun. Like decorative traverse rods, but less expensive, they'll be a full-time accent in your room. Finishes run the gambit — bright or antique brass, satin black or bronze, antique white or walnut. Mix or match the rings to shift the emphasis around.

John Hartley, photography. Marcus Saxer, design.

92A (left). Diners look at sky and trees, but no one looks at them. And at a problem window, too! Shirred curtains on spring pressure rods (page 122) expose the multi-frames. Rings repeat the walnut finish as they hold side panels on a fabric-covered pole (page 119).

93A (top). A light, sure hand framed this alcove setting. Yours, too, could be as delicate — just use this as a guide. Slivers of bright brass (page 118) support the lace cafes, don't overpower them. And note the rings are white. The valance here is custommade. A ruffle could be sewn at home.

Hedrich-Blessing, photography. Adelaide Radcliffe, design.

93B (right). It's hard to be untidy in a room with so much space to put away. Louvered panels can cover the TV to encourage conversation. And cabinets hide the radiators, too. A simple window treatment, on spring pressure rods (page 122), helps to balance the rich red in this room.

Curtains leave the kitchen

Measuring information on page 68

Kent Oppenheimer, photography. Mattraw-Vickman Interiors, design.

One of window fashion's "newest" styles was born back in the 1900's. Curtains — lace and otherwise. And used with practicality, they merit the revival.

In fact, curtains have a single drawback. They don't draw. They're a stationary treatment. Tie them back and the window can be opened, but the room will be on stage. Hang them straight and gain some privacy, but lose the air and view. Open the window and they'll blow. So balance them against draw sheers before you make a choice.

Cost can be a factor. You have a range of curtains ready-made. And even if you've never sewn, you can make curtains with great confidence. Or trim the ones you buy.

If curtains are your choice, pick up another trend. Shirr them over fat wood poles or cafe rods. It gives new dimension to the top, and pretty ends of rods that show add a designer-did-it look. See how to do it on page 75.

For more variety, try something other than a single curtain on a single curtain rod. Use a double rod for a valance over curtains. Or for two pairs, one tied-back, one hanging straight. Or for a pair of crisscross panels.

Don't worry about rods to fit your windows. There are those for corners, bays and bows. Ones that snuggle close for use on doors. Ones to go inside the frame. Still more kinds to use for valances or canopies.

94A (left). Sliding windows live in many homes. These are gently tailored. Two pairs of curtains — they could be ready-mades — are hung on one long rod (page 122) to make them seem continuous. And with the look well-softened, shades are used for privacy.

95A (top right). Look beyond the pink parade and see an ordinary window stretching tall. Shades and curtains hang up high, and poufing panels create a slim illusion. Shirr them over a wood pole (page 119) and paint the ends to match cheery gingham checks.

95B (far right top). The best of yesterday lives with a pattern mix that's very good today. At the window, yards and yards of lovely lace. Ends of the wood pole (page 119) extend about a foot beyond the window to support a velvet scarf, just as they used to do.

95C (lower right). This double-curtained wall might be glass or multi-windows or even merely plaster. There's no telling if the treatment doesn't open. Buttery underpanels hang on short projection curtain rods (page 122). But the pretty print is shirred on a bright brass rod (page 118) to repeat the bedstead.

Courtesy, Window Shade Mfrs. Assoc. Dorothy Baker Billings, design.

Harold Davis, photography. Nadine Russel and Joy Koch, design.

Kent Oppennheimer, photography. Joyce Grossman Interiors, design.

Beautiful, practical, versatile, durable woven woods

Measuring information on page 69

Paulus Leeser, photography. John Maurer, Inc., design.

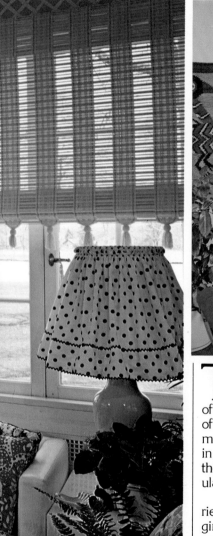

96A (far left). In this eclectic room. an action mix of furnishings plays well against the quiet backdrop of the woven woods (pages 124, 125). Choose an open weave like this to welcome in the light. And see how a Roman shade works on the door far left, as well as at the windows.

97A (top left). Sun country life is great, but to keep your cooled-down air inside, there's nothing better than a shade of woven wood. The more yarn and the tighter the weave, the more the insulation. But use sun-bright colors if you like. This is LaPaz white (pages 124, 125).

97B (lower left). Odd-sized, offbeat windows are no problem if you use shades of woven wood. They're made to fit precisely. Here, Saddleback walnut (pages 124, 125) has been used — its earthy tones, a natural in this room of many browns.

The latest things in window wear are made of woven wood. Shades, of course, but also other kinds of coverings. And while they more than earn their keep in practicality, appearance is the "why" behind their popular appeal.

Whenever texture marries color, exciting things begin. When it's done with yarn and wood, the look is fresh and natural, and color can run free — from sharp, bright hues to quiet monochromes.

Weave is another good-looks factor. Some are almost light as lace, others thick with nubby yarns. Pick yours for the sun screen and the privacy you need.

Roman shades are by far the leading style, but there are many other things to do with woven wood. Have shades that roll just like their fabric relatives. Or double-folds that close from either top or bottom. Or have draw draperies, cafes or folding doors. Or even put your woven woods on walls.

At windows, any shade style's practical because it exposes or covers all the glass and needs no wall space to stack back. And woven woods enhance most any room.

You'll also find them easy to care for. Just vacuum periodically. Their beauty's tough enough to last for years.

Insulation? Woven wood works hard to keep out heat and cold and help you cut down noise.

Altogether, it's small wonder that woven woods are the newest window wonder.

Accordion pleats for draperies

Use Accordia-Fold® or Archifold® ... custom drapery heading systems

98A (above). Draperies of woven wood stack back more compactly when used with Archifold. Here, you see them partly opened. The installation's two-way draw—could also be one-way. The rich, ripe colors of Morocco (pages 124, 125) add zest to this pleasant room.

98B (left). Here Accordia-Fold is used with a wispy, see-through fabric. This makes the pleating less precise—it may be a look you like. But soft or knife-edged, Accordia-Fold pleated panels still stack back much more compactly than panels made with conventional pinch pleats.

99A (right). Modern's nicer now than modern ever was before. That's because, today, strong lines are played against a host of softer ones. See the rug and all the natural accessories used here. Note, too, the sculptured look of Accordia-Fold draperies. They open to uncover most of this glass wall.

If yours is the kind of home, and you're the kind of person, for a something-different look in draperies, think about accordion pleats. The look is slim and trim and tailored. The function is conventional. Like pinch-pleated draperies, these panels are controlled by cords.

But knife-sharp pleats give fabrics — and woven woods — a freshly modern feel. And draperies are as neat and natty from the outside looking in as from the inside looking out.

Because they also fold compactly, accordion pleats stack back in roughly half the space as panels of pinch pleats. So narrow windows have a better glass-and-fabric balance and more light shines through a wall of glass.

There's still one more advantage. Draperies for Accordia-Fold and Archifold heading systems snap on and off the rod. No hooks to tug at fabric.

Treatments this unusual must be custom made — both rod and draperies — so not all Kirsch dealers handle them. Look for a store or shop that makes custom draperies, or a designer who can find them for you. And ask about them by their proper names — Accordia-Fold or Archifold drapery heading systems.

A rippled look for draperies

Use Ripplefold®...custom drapery heading system

If pinch pleats just aren't quite your look, try a soft, new dress for windows — unpressed folds that add a sculptural dimension. Closed, they gently flow and undulate. Open, they stack back into classic columns.

Whether fabric or woven wood, treatments made with Ripplefold are in every sense draw draperies, with all their practicality. You operate them with a cord. But they outdo pinch pleats in several ways.

There's less fabric in a "ripple" than in a triple pleat. So there's less to stack back when your draperies are open. That means Ripplefold covers as completely, but uncovers more compactly.

And ripples are ripples from both sides of the glass. They look as tidy from your porch or patio as from the room inside.

Hanging draperies made with Ripplefold is fast. They snap in place — no hooks. But when the panels are unsnapped, they're flat. Easy to clean or launder. The folds re-form automatically as you snap the panels back in place.

Ripplefold is a custom system — both draperies and the traverse track. Look for it by name in a store or shop that custom makes their draperies and handles the Kirsch brand. Or have a designer specify it for your home.

100A (left). The stripes of pillow ticking stress Ripplefold's unpleated columns. Each panel is a one-way draw so windows can be covered or uncovered individually — and see how little space they need to stack back at the sides. More ticking turns the cornerwall, confirming that the windows are one unit.

101A (above). The ins and outs of Ripplefold are mixable–crisp with modern, classic with traditional. And its compact stackback comes in handy at a sliding door. Open, much more glass is bared. This treatment is a one-way draw done with woven wood pattern, Hondo (pages 124, 125).

Flattering flat panels

Use Paneltrac®...custom drapery heading system

Modernage, photography.

102A *(left). At home, or somewhere else, offices respond to the no-frills, tailored look of Paneltrac. For warmth, as well as noise control, try the texture of a woven wood. This treatment's one-way draw, done with El Dorado in mahogany (pages 124, 125).*

103A *(right). Who knows what hides behind this wall-wide sweep. If it's all glass, most can be uncovered with the panels open. If it's mismatched windows, no one sees. But everyone's aware that the fabric is a handsome one when it's hung free of fullness.*

In Japan, this look's achieved with sliding shoji screens. Here, it's often done with Paneltrac — big impact for your windows, or for room dividers elsewhere.

Flat panels can blend into the background or demand attention as a wall-wide mural. That depends on fabric. But no folds break up the pattern of a print or the texture of a woven wood.

Flat panels cover the most area with the least yardage. And because they work like sliding screens, they stack back most compactly.

Flat panels are hung or taken down in minutes. Clean or launder easily. Store in very little space.

That's what they do. "How" is the clever part. Paneltrac has Velcro® surfaced sliders. More Velcro holds fabric to these sliders, which are pulled with a baton.

To close the sliding panels over glass, pull the first. The others follow automatically. To bare the glass, again you pull the first. The others will stack back behind it. There's no floor track at all.

Paneltrac is custom tailored to your windows and to the width of fabric you choose. That's why you won't find it everywhere. Look for a store that makes custom draperies and ask for Paneltrac by name. Or have a designer do it for you.

®T.M., Kirsch Co.   ®T.M., Velcro Corp.

Max Eckert, photography. Sharon Carvell, design.

Switch control for drawing draperies

Use Electrac®...electromagnetic traverse rodding

104A (left). It's not your average window, but it's a natural for Electrac. Draperies this wide and long could be hard to close, but anyone can flip a switch. Both the sheers and overdraperies are electromagnetically controlled, can be operated independently.

105A (above). At a high, wide wall of glass like this, it's easier to flip a switch than draw a cord. And Electrac is ideal with sheers. Its electromagnetic motors are concealed within the rod. No need to find a place to hide a motor mounted on the wall.

Electrac's not another look for draperies, but it surely is a nice, new way to make them work. Instead of pulling cords, you just flip a switch, like turning on a light. Electromagnetic motors in the rod draw the draperies.

Why a switch instead of cords? Because it can be practical. For very wide or long or heavy draperies. For windows way up high where cords are difficult to reach. And if you have an invalid at home, Electrac lets them draw their draperies from bed. Of course, that's awfully nice for anyone.

The switch goes where it's most convenient. Even in another room, so you can draw your draperies from an entry or a hall.

If you're building new, the wiring can go inside the walls, but you can add Electrac anytime you like. Literally, the rod plugs into a standard household outlet. That means no motors on the wall. They're inside the rod itself. And still it's slim and trim.

Draperies needn't be made special. Use the pinch-pleated ones you have. But if you like, Electrac can be used with Ripplefold or Accordia-Fold. Read about them on pages 98 to 101.

Electrac is sold only by specially approved Kirsch dealers. If you'd like the name of one near you, write to Kirsch Company.

IT ALL
BEGINS WITH
PROPER DRAPERY
HARDWARE

AFTER YOU'VE DECIDED WHAT YOU WANT TO DO WITH YOUR WINDOWS, THE NEXT STEP IS FINDING OUT HOW TO DO IT. HAPPILY, THAT'S ALMOST ALWAYS SIMPLE. JUST REMEMBER, IT TAKES THE RIGHT SELECTION OF DRAPERY HARDWARE. THE RODS MAY BE BEAUTIFUL, AND INTENDED TO SHOW. OR THEY MAY DO THEIR WORK BEHIND THE SCENE. THE NEXT PAGES WILL HELP TO FILL YOU IN. IF YOU HAVE A SPECIAL PROBLEM, ASK YOUR STORE OR YOUR DESIGNER TO ASSIST YOU.

Traditionally beautiful Chateau®

Purists may not approve the broad-use term "traditional," but they applaud its gracious look. And whether you're exclusively devoted to one period of design, or prefer to mix up several with an eclectic hand, you'll find Chateau belongs. It's a gentle window accent.

Fluting creates highlights on the body of the rod. Up-sized rings have a sculptured profile, too. And acorn finials are straight from classical design.

For coordination with your fabrics and your color scheme, Chateau traverse and cafe rods come in an antiqued brass-look finish or in a white antiqued with gold. There are holdbacks in both finishes and tieback chains in antique brass and white.

108A (left). Strong elements of Early American and a mosaic of natural materials make this room relaxing. A Chateau traverse rod spans and draws attention to the pretty picture window. The table, topped with pheasant feathers, and the bookcase just beyond are both the twist-together kind (pages 130, 131).

109A (top right). Coordinate colors and contrast textures for this sophisticated look. A super silky fabric's used for spread and draperies. It's played against the rush seat chairs and shade of woven wood (the pattern is Gordola). The window's even more important when finished with a Chateau traverse rod.

Modernage, photography.

1⅜" adjustable traverse; antique brass or antique white

1" adjustable traverse; antique brass or antique white

1³⁄₁₆" adjustable cafe; antique brass or antique white
Matching cafe rings sold separately.

Sherwood...steel that's dressed to look like wood

Hedrich-Blessing, photography. Irwin Blietz, developer.

110A (far left). Textures help to make this room — nubby rug, smooth woods, parquetry of wall and floor. The handsome sliding door is treated as a window. See how just a touch of trim leads the eye up to the Sherwood traverse rod.

111A (left). Earthy naturals and comfortable seating make an inviting conversation area. Floor-length draperies seem to stretch the strip window to a bigger size. And a walnut finished Sherwood traverse rod blends with paneling.

1⅜" adjustable traverse; walnut or white finish.

1³⁄₁₆" adjustable cafe; walnut finish. Matching cafe rings sold separately.

1" adjustable traverse; walnut finish.

1⅜" adjustable hand traverse; walnut or white finish.

The wood pole look is in. In style. Informal. Innovative. Sherwood gives you all of this, but goes wood one better because it's made of steel.

Hung properly, Sherwood's stronger than wood, less apt to sag or warp. And you don't have to saw to size. Sherwood rods adjust.

Going wide? Sherwood's better than a pole. Its half-round rings slide right over rod supports. Full rings on a wood pole won't. That means panels must be narrower in width.

When you use a Sherwood traverse rod, your draperies draw with cords. Fabric panels on wood poles must be drawn by hand. And those cords are more than just convenient, they help to keep your fabrics clean.

Sherwood traverse and cafe rods come in walnut and white finishes with holdbacks to match.

Atavio...from country to contemporary, even oriental

A tavio doesn't give you just one look, or even two. Its squared-off shape and choice of finials and finishes let you "hand tailor" its big and bold design.

In the store, you'll find Atavio black or bronze finished traverse and cafe rods packed with tapering square finials. Use these in informal or oriental settings. But if you'd like your traverse rod to have a "lighter" look, add Monterrey finials, sold separately. This open fleur-de-lis is slightly dressier, on the more formal side.

Using holdbacks or tiebacks? You'll find them in black or bronze to match.

112A (left). The crucial difference between understating and ignoring is demonstrated here. The mullioned window is exquisite, but without draperies, would seem to be undressed. Atavio is bold enough to be in scale but far from fussy looking. Professionally smocked drapery headings add another unpretentious touch.

113A (above right). From headboard to pillows to duster to window, this blossomy magic's done with sheets — and that means a most modest cost. Short, print draperies bloom above a floor-length panel. You'll need an Atavio and a conventional rod for each window in your room.

Foto Graphics, Inc., photography. Morley Smith, design

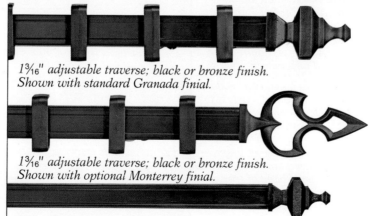

1³⁄₁₆" *adjustable traverse; black or bronze finish. Shown with standard Granada finial.*

1³⁄₁₆" *adjustable traverse; black or bronze finish. Shown with optional Monterrey finial.*

1³⁄₁₆" *adjustable cafe; black or bronze finish. Matching cafe rings sold separately.*

Vintage®...where finish makes the difference

For versatility, Vintage is the one. It's a classical design that holds to no one mood of furnishings. Instead, you'll want to choose the finish that will play up other metal accents in your room.

In pewter, you'll find Vintage swings from comfortable contemporary to fairly formal Federal. In either of its pair of "golden" finishes, it can smile with quiet dignity or become as friendly as Early American.

Finish aside, you're sure to like the way the fluted rod gives you a play of light and shadow. And the way the super smoothness of its finials (those decorative end pieces) contrasts with the fluting.

Vintage comes in traverse rod styles only. In finishes that simulate soft brass, warmer antique gold or silky pewter. There are matching holdbacks and tieback chains in all three finishes.

114A (above). There's a lot to be said for dining graciously. And quite a lot for the gracious look of this window in this room. A pewter finish traverse rod holds the overdraperies, while a conventional traverse (pages 120, 121) controls the imported undersheers.

115A (right). Hard-edge modern may need chrome (pages 116, 117), but contemporary lives best with softer finishes and colors. Here, pewter gleams and glows and makes its presence known quite subtly. See how a simple band of trim ties plain white draperies to the total color scheme.

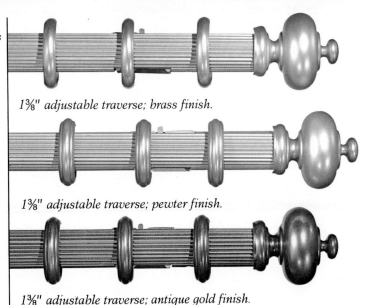

1⅜" adjustable traverse; brass finish.

1⅜" adjustable traverse; pewter finish.

1⅜" adjustable traverse; antique gold finish.

If "today" is a look you like, try Mod-Rod®

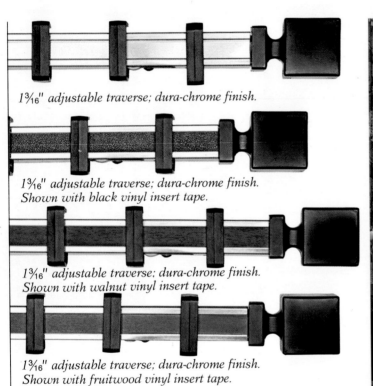

1³⁄₁₆" *adjustable traverse; dura-chrome finish.*

1³⁄₁₆" *adjustable traverse; dura-chrome finish. Shown with black vinyl insert tape.*

1³⁄₁₆" *adjustable traverse; dura-chrome finish. Shown with walnut vinyl insert tape.*

1³⁄₁₆" *adjustable traverse; dura-chrome finish. Shown with fruitwood vinyl insert tape.*

Foto Graphics, Inc., photography. Morley Smith, design

If you're into clean, crisp lines and great splashes of strong color, other decorative drapery hardware styles may seem "over decorative" to you. But not the really honest geometrics of this one. It's specifically designed for modernists.

Use this streak of chrome-like metal as it is...boldly rectangular with inky black rings and squared-off finials. Or strip self-adhesive vinyl tape along its shiny face. Choose to use black, walnut or fruitwood.

Mod-Rod's available only as a traverse rod. Its dura-chrome finish resists tarnish. Optional vinyl tape strips are sold separately.

116A (above). Certainly, use sheets! These days there's such a wide variety of patterns that no one would know they were intended for the bedroom. And their pre-hemming saves home-sewer's time. These gain in stature by being hung on a Mod-Rod faced with vinyl fruitwood tape.

117A (right). Reds are redder, blacks are inkier, when played against pure white. It's a most decisive color scheme. Reflective finishes abound. The window wears a rod of chrome, and draperies are flashed with metallic threads. At the inset window, they're hung on a Superfine traverse rod (pages 120, 121).

Bold as brass

Harold Davis, photography. Habitational Designs, design.

You can't say brass is back because it's always had its share of fans, but it certainly has more of them these days. This bright and shiny finish lives well in many settings, and that's why it's on the move again.

Simplicity's the word that best describes this style and its unpretentiousness is absolutely right with Early American, Country or any provincial type of furnishings. It's also ideal with eclectic and has traditional appeal.

Kirsch makes traverse rods that look like brass — but won't ever tarnish — in two diameters. Use Heritage at wider windows or where you want a little extra "gleam." Use Galaxy at smaller ones or for more subtlety.

Cafe rods also come in differing diameters. Great for standard cafe curtains, you can use them for shirred curtains, too, and just their pretty tips will show.

There are matching cafe rings, of course. Tiebacks and holdbacks if you wish.

118A (right). Shimmering brass accents add balance to this semi-formal room. Multi-paneled draperies help with symmetry. Hang them from a single traverse rod. To do this type of treatment, each intermediate panel needs two overlaps. The two end panels need one overlap and one return.

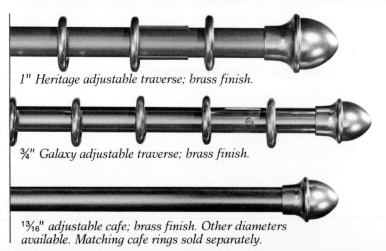

1" Heritage adjustable traverse; brass finish.

¾" Galaxy adjustable traverse; brass finish.

¹³⁄₁₆" adjustable cafe; brass finish. Other diameters available. Matching cafe rings sold separately.

Take to the woods

Wood poles work. And they're especially helpful if you're imaginative.

Paint them, stain them, fabric cover them. Mix or match the rings. Or don't use rings at all. Shirr curtains over them. Tie macrame to them. Hang flat panels.

But do remember, if you use them as you would a curtain rod, your treatment will be stationary. And if you use them as a traverse rod, you'll have to hand draw panels, so the fabric may be soiled when you pull it.

Kirsch poles come in white, walnut and natural, with a choice of two finials. For use over sheer curtains, buy the special brackets which hold both pole and curtain rod.

119A (right). Eclectic settings, like this one with its trompe l'oeil breakfront, grow more exciting when draperies have a "different" look. Here, twin windows wear fabric shirred on fat wood poles, and an old idea's revived, as skirts sweep wide upon the floor.

Max Eckert, photography. Evelyn McCabe, design.

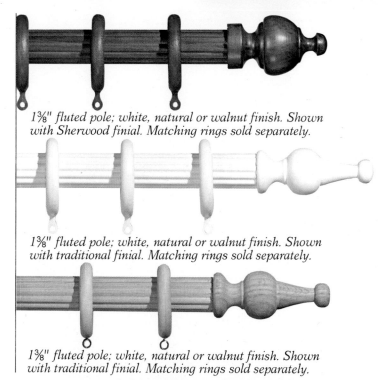

1⅜" fluted pole; white, natural or walnut finish. Shown with Sherwood finial. Matching rings sold separately.

1⅜" fluted pole; white, natural or walnut finish. Shown with traditional finial. Matching rings sold separately.

1⅜" fluted pole; white, natural or walnut finish. Shown with traditional finial. Matching rings sold separately.

Conventional does not mean commonplace

Decorative traverse rods show all the time. But, closed, draperies hide conventional traverse rods. Either style can help you do a handsome treatment, and both adjust to fit most any window width.

The conventional traverse rods you'll find in stores are one or two-way draw. A two-way draw closes two separate panels in the center of a window. A one-way draw pulls one panel all one way across the glass.

Conventional traverse rods come singly or in a choice of combination sets — two traverse rods, or a traverse and a curtain rod. You can add a valance rod, sold separately, to a single rod or set.

Most conventional rods are white. Some are walnut finished and they're great at blending into paneled walls.

If you've a special window problem and can't find a packaged rod to solve it, your Kirsch dealer can order custom cut-to-measure rods. They solve a multitude of problems. And while not truly expensive, they can be worth their weight in gold if you're facing complications.

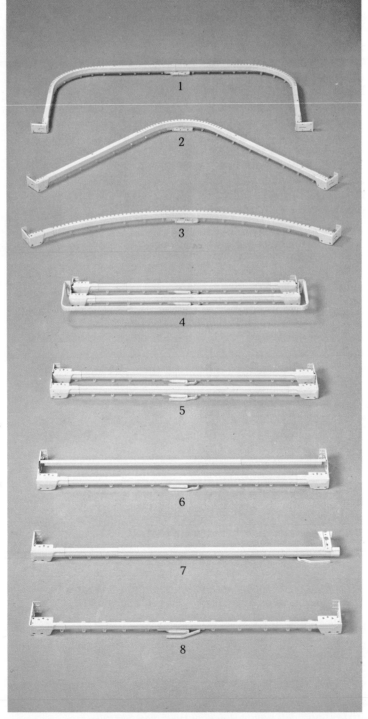

120A (left). No. 1, cut-to-measure traverse rod for rectangular bay. No. 2, cut-to-measure traverse rod for corner window. No. 3, cut-to-measure traverse rod for bow window. No. 4, double traverse rod with valance rod. No. 5, double traverse rod. No. 6, traverse and curtain rod set. No. 7, one-way draw traverse rod. No. 8, two-way draw traverse rod.

121A (top right). Here's a triple rod at work. Begin with a traverse-curtain set, then add a valance rod. Why a traverse rod when the center-tied panels don't draw? Simply because draperies with pinch pleats, hidden or not, don't drape as well if you put them on a curtain rod.

121B (top far right). Here's a case for cut-to-measure. Since this secluded view needs little screening off, the draperies were never meant to draw. They're on short lengths of ceiling-mounted rodding. Fabric on the wall above unifies the corner — free-hanging "tabs" are an inventive plus.

121C (right). Two double traverse rod sets tie this bow and sliding door together. White rods are scarcely seen against the painted wall, while walnut finished ones blend into the paneling.

Virginia Frankel, design.

Leland Lee, photography. Carole Eichen, design.

Hedrich-Blessing, photography. Blietz-Valenti, developer.

Behold the quiet, simple curtain rod

There's nothing very complicated about a curtain rod, but you may not realize just how many kinds there are — each designed to do a special job.

There are single and double curtain rods. Rods for corners, rods for bays. Those that fit up tight to doors and those that project for valances and canopies. Rods without brackets—springs keep them in place inside a window frame. Even cut-to-measure rods. All simple, basic, inexpensive and made to help you with your windows.

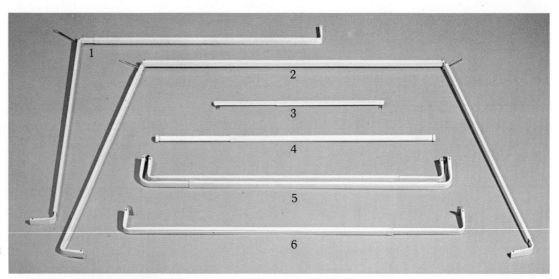

122A (above right). No. 1, curtain rod for corner window. No. 2, curtain rod for bay window. No. 3, sash rod. No. 4, spring pressure curtain rod. No. 5, double curtain rod. No. 6, single curtain rod.

122B (right). Taste, not money, makes this room inviting. Wicker brings the outside in and a carefree print breeds fresh, free unity. Ruffled curtains hang inside the snowy frame on a spring pressure curtain rod.

Look to the little things

S ome accessories are beautiful. Like silky rope tiebacks and chains of multi-finished metal. Or ornately sculpted holdbacks. It's just like choosing jewelry.

Others aren't so pretty — they do their work behind the scenes. Like a variety of drapery hooks. The label on your Kirsch rod box tells you which kind to use. And rings for cafe rods clip on, sew on or hold a drapery hook.

Sewing? Weights help control the hems of draperies, make them hang more gracefully. Buckram or Easypleat® tape can help you make the headings. And Kir-Flex eyelet rodding bends to almost any shape — does the difficult and different.

So if you're looking for something beautiful to see or to sew with, look to Kirsch accessories.

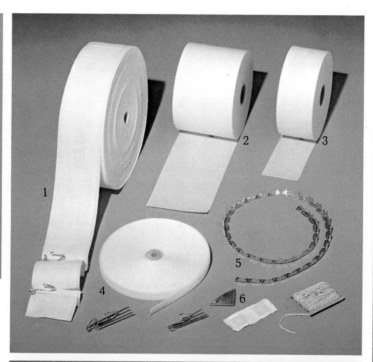

123A (far left). Hooks and rings and mounting screws may not be the most exciting part of planning window treatments, but they're certainly essential. The box which holds your rod will recommend the proper rings or hooks — and it also holds the mounting screws suitable for most installations.

123B (left). No. 1 is Easypleat tape and hooks. Nos. 2 and 3 are buckram for use in headings. No. 4 is Velcro fastening tape. No. 5 is flexible Kir-Flex rodding and No. 6 shows drapery weights of various types.

123C (below left). Just a few of the many accessories which can do so much to add a finishing touch to many lovely windows.

Shades of woven wood

124A (above). Canopied shades aren't just for kitchens. Although festive there, they're also great for other rooms. Witness this den window wearing Yucatan walnut. Any pattern that's heavy with yarn can be trimmed with self-tied tassels.

124B (left). Here's proof that rough, tough window problems give in gracefully to shades of woven wood. Valances are custom fitted to the slant, or to an arch. This shade is Roman style, done in Nob Hill walnut.

125A (right). You say you want to match a tortoise shell precisely. Or the colors in an heirloom quilt or imported paisley shawl. It can be done — it has been here. Dramatically. Shades look more trimly tailored when hung inside the window frame.

Choosing a woven wood window treatment is a little different than selecting rods and draperies. You may find it even easier, especially if you rely upon a store to help.

Of course, it all starts with your windows. Any windows, except bows, are likely candidates. The common kinds, but also arches, slants, corners, bays — the unusual shapes respond to shades of woven wood.

Your first decision is the pattern. Kirsch makes dozens of woven wood designs, in a variety of colors. You may want to add a valance, with or without trim. Or a canopy. Again, you'll have many styles to choose from.

Specific types of shades may have somewhat unfamiliar names — Roman, roller, double-fold, cord and pulley, etc. But don't be concerned with terminology. Just tell your dealer what you want your shade to do. He'll know which kind you need.

And don't forget you can have woven wood made into draperies, cafe curtains, etc. Even use it for wall covering.

If you'd like the name of a dealer or designer in your area who can help with woven woods, contact Kirsch Company.

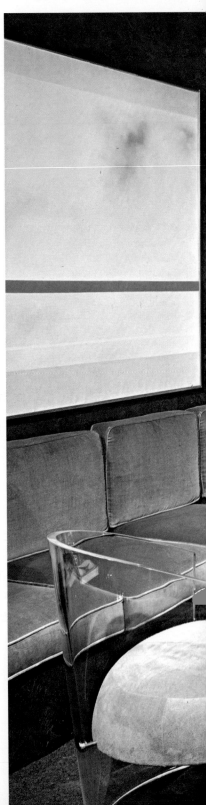

Modernage, photography.

Modernage, photography.

Paulus Leeser, photography. Formica Corp., design.

OTHER IDEAS TO BRIGHTEN UP YOUR HOME

THERE'S ANOTHER SUBJECT IN THESE PAGES. OTHER WAYS TO HAVE A NICER AND MORE INTERESTING HOME. THERE ARE SHELVES TO HANG ON WALLS. SHELVES THAT TWIST TOGETHER INTO FURNITURE. FRESH ACCENTS FOR THE BATH AND OTHER PLACES. ART TO HANG MOST ANYWHERE. ALL BEAUTIFUL. ALL AFFORDABLE. SO TAKE JUST A MINUTE NOW. SEE HOW THESE THINGS, TOO, MIGHT HELP ENHANCE A HOME.

126A (left). A striking window wears draw draperies and a Roman shade of woven wood—the pattern's Honeycomb. Also adding to the room are a handsome pair of prints, "Sunlit Blossoms" and "Sunlit Daisies," a twist-together table and a rug that's painted on the floor.

A choice of ways to shelve it

128A (left). A special shelf is wide enough to hold your sound equipment. Compactly solves that ever-present "where?" Or if you'd like, it makes a handy mini-desk.

128B (above). It doesn't take much space or money to turn a small hall wall into a showoff spot for handsome things. The scrolled brackets used for this arrangement give shelves a dressed-up look.

129A (right). Shelving fills this long and empty sofa wall. Massed, small items gain importance. When snuggled close together, shelves need no unifying standards on the wall. Also note the pretty treatment of the bay. Pinch-pleated panels are on three traverse rods (pages 120, 121), shirred curtains on spring pressure rods.

Collectibles are a vital, and often inexpensive, way to decorate today. Be they books or baskets, put them out to be enjoyed. The proper place may be on wall-hung shelving.

Once, wall arrangements were difficult to plan. Were you going to hit or miss wall studding? Now, that problem's solved by shelving planned to mount on 16" centers, the standard studding in most homes. Gone are ragged-edge arrangements.

And today's "furniture for walls" can be formal or informal. It changes with your choice of bracket styles. Vinyl finishes look for all the world like wood, but smile through a lot more wear and tear.

And, of course, this kind of shelving's flexible. Space shelves close or far apart. Use them one way now, another later on. Buy a wall-full or a shelf or two. Add to when you will. For the name of a shelving dealer near you, drop Kirsch Company a line.

Furniture with a twist of your wrist

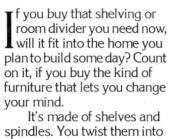

If you buy that shelving or room divider you need now, will it fit into the home you plan to build some day? Count on it, if you buy the kind of furniture that lets you change your mind.

It's made of shelves and spindles. You twist them into end tables, bookcases, room dividers, stereo centers, etc. If you change your mind or home, just twist them into something else.

Takes no tools, no glue, no finishing. Makes no mess and goes together fast. Even costs less because you do the assembly.

Spindles come in several styles and lengths. The shelves, in different finishes, are all vinyl laminated to shrug off most household spills. If you'd like to see it for yourself, write Kirsch for the name of a nearby dealer.

130A (left). Every home should have an entry. If yours doesn't, make one. This shelving, filled with pretties, makes the space break nicely. Use it to section off a bedroom for two children, a dining from a living area, use it any place you'd like to have a wall.

131A (above top). Want to get it all together? Here's a spot for all your sound equipment, plus TV. Compact, convenient and attractive. Traditionally designed spindles enhance many settings.

131B (above bottom). It's a neat, little table now, but it might be the beginning of a room divider you'll have later. This kind of furniture you add-to anytime. Slightly oriental spindles work well with contemporary furnishings.

Crafty ways with art

Almost apologetically, it's said, "I don't know much about art, but I know what I like." Well, that's all you need to know to enjoy it in your home. And no other single element speaks so instantly of you.

The kind of art you like — reproductions of the masters, modern abstracts, old inn signs or an eclectic mix — matters not at all. Just as long as it delights you every day. Choose it for this alone.

Then, let it help you with some other things. For instance, a painting can set your color scheme. Or fill in for missing furniture — use a grouping as a headboard, one large piece to warm a long, cold wall.

Where? Anywhere. There's space in every room from kitchen to the bath. A small print in an unexpected place can make a big impression. And there are paintings specially sized to "fit" above a sofa or a fireplace.

One large piece packs a decorating wallop, but so does a group of smaller things. To group, gather your "collection" on a floor space equal to the wall. Plot it there before you hang a thing.

Lighting's no cause for concern. The kind of art you'll likely use takes to diffused, indirect light. In recommending this, one highly respected and practical collector says, "A home is not a gallery."

Today's techniques give you excellent posters, prints, etchings, silk screens, even original oils, at prices you can easily afford. If you'd like to know more, write Kirsch Company for the name of a dealer in your area.

132A (above). Think of frames as also being furniture, enhancing both the art and total room. Here, Vanguard prints, "Sally" and "Dawn," respond to light and open lattice frames.

133A (right). The color all comes from "Fish Kites." The black, the creamy whites, the brick. And how well balanced this room is! Against black, the painting is an instant focal point. Lots of white adds counterbalance. Notice how the stripes of the drapery panels repeat the ribbons of the kites.

Small beauties for the bath...
and more

There are small things that every bathroom needs — towel bars or rings, soap dishes, toothbrush and tissue holders, shower bars, etc. If you use the ordinary kind, they function, but that's all. So why not add the beauty of the same small things, designer styled? They work as hard and last as long, but dress up your bath or powder room while doing it.

These little things are also very much at home elsewhere. Pretty drawer knobs and pulls can help old chests and cabinets look like new. Electrical switch and outlet plates are handsome anywhere. Towel bars are fine for kitchens and a magnifying mirror is welcome in the bedroom.

Kirsch's little things come in plain and fancy styles, in several finishes. Write for the name of a dealer near you.

134A (left). Pinch-pleated draperies at a tub enclosure? Only with a dual-track shower bar. One track has hooks for a liner. The other, rings for pleated panels. Use draperies that match those at your bathroom windows. And match the drapery hardware, too. This is a Chateau shower bar. Rods are on pages 108, 109.

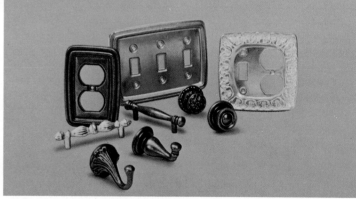

135A (left). Coordinating little accent items make for a big impression. Here, antique white Chateau is used for pulls, switch plate, toothbrush holder and the make-up mirror.

135B (below left). Kitchen towels are so pretty nowadays, they should be hung to show. They'll look their best on a bar that's handsome, too. This one, and the drawer pulls, are Concord in a casual chrome finish.

135C (below). Anywhere around the house! Hooks and knobs and pulls and plates. Choose them in simply styled Concord or the more ornate Chateau.

A checklist for window treatment planning

If you're seriously interested in planning the most attractive and practical window treatments for your home — and in obtaining the most value for your money — now is the time to review any sections of this book which apply to your particular situation.

Then, answer these questions. Let them guide the way to a shopping list. In the long run, you'll save time and effort.

About the window and the room
1. Where is the window?
 Living room
 Dining room
 Family room
 Bedroom
 Kitchen
 Bath
 Other
2. In general, what type of furnishings are or will be in the room? The window should "tie-in."
 Pure period: Victorian, Louis XIV, etc.
 Traditional
 Casual
 Contemporary
 Eclectic
3. What is your color scheme? If you intend to change it, decide how.
 If only the window treatment will be changed, decide which color you want to use there.
4. Does the fabric need to be a special type?
 Especially long-wearing
 Resistant to sun
 Stable in humid situations
 Easy care
5. Does the room have ample light? Do you need to or want to uncover all the glass at times?
6. How is the view? Think about it on a bad day as well as on a pretty one. Think about it from the outside in as well as from the inside out.
7. Do you want the window to be a focal point or would you prefer it blend into the background?
8. Is the room "open" to other rooms, so that several windows should be related, if not identical, in their treatment?
9. Would you feel more comfortable in the room if you could have complete privacy at times?
10. What direction does the window face? Is there ever need for sun or light control?
 For protection of furnishings and fabrics
 For temperature control
11. Will the window ever be opened to help adjust inside temperature? Will it ever need to be completely covered to block out drafts and help save energy?
12. Is outside noise ever an annoyance?
13. Are you happy with the window's shape or would you prefer to change it?
 Make it look wider
 Make it look narrower
 Make it look taller
 Make it look shorter
14. Are there any architectural or physical factors that would affect the window's treatment? Is there room for normal stackback?
 Wall space to both sides
 Large pieces of furniture
 Radiators
 Window air conditioners
15. Realistically, what is your window treatment budget? What type of treatment fits it best?
 Sew-it-yourself
 Ready-mades
 Made-to-measure
 Custom-mades

About the kind of window
1. What kind of window are you treating? Does anything about it need some special sort of handling?
 Glass wall
 Sliding door
 Picture
 Multiple: how many, how far apart
 Corner
 Bay
 Bow
 Problem: see question 3
2. If it opens, and you will be opening it, how does it open?
3. What kind of problem window do you have?
 Clerestory
 Slanted
 Arched
 Ranch or strip
 Dormer
 Small
 Tall and narrow
 Inswinging casement
 Door
4. Will your problem respond to any readily available type of treatment? Or will you need something special?

About the treatment in general
1. Based on the things you now know about your window, where do you want to put your drapery hardware?
 On the ceiling
 On the wall
 On the window frame: not recommended for draw draperies
 Inside the window frame: not recommended for draw draperies
2. What length do you want your treatment to be?
 To the floor
 To the bottom of the window frame
 To the window sill: recommended primarily for use when rods are hung inside the frame

About the window treatment style and measuring for it
If you've answered all the questions up to here, you're ready to select the style of window treatment that meets the most of your requirements. You'll find them shown on pages 78 through 105.

The information on pages 66 through 69, details how to measure for each specific style. Do take your measurements with a steel rule or a yardstick; cloth tapes will stretch.

If you're measuring a wide expanse of glass or going from the ceiling to the floor, measure at each end of the window and one other point in between. The ceiling, the floor or the window may not be exactly level.

And don't forget to make all the necessary allowances for clearance of ceiling, floor, valances, etc.

Now make your shopping list
You have all the facts and figures, so it's fine to make a shopping list. You'll find the basic elements for the most popular treatments here.

1. Single draw draperies
One traverse rod: decorative or conventional style; one or two-way draw.

One pair or one panel of draperies depending on rod draw.

Tiebacks if desired
Drapery hooks
Valance, if desired. If using valance, purchase a valance-traverse rod combination set.

2. Double draw draperies
Two traverse rods. If a decorative rod is used over a conventional rod, also purchase combination brackets. If both rods are to be conventional, purchase a combination double traverse rod set. Rods may be one or two-way draw.

Two pairs or two panels of draperies depending on rod draw.

Tiebacks if desired
Drapery hooks
Valance if desired. If using valance, purchase a valance rod kit.

3. Draw draperies with woven wood shades
One traverse rod: decora-

tive or conventional style; one or two-way draw.

One pair or one panel of draperies depending on rod draw.

Tiebacks if desired
Drapery hooks
One woven wood shade

4. Draw draperies with curtains
One traverse and one curtain rod. If a decorative traverse rod is used, purchase a Series 3700 utility curtain rod. If both rods are to be conventional, purchase a combination traverse-curtain rod set. Traverse rods may be one or two-way draw.

One pair or one panel of draperies depending on rod draw.

One pair or one panel of curtains

Tiebacks if desired
Drapery hooks
Valance if desired. If using valance, purchase valance rod kit.

5. Draw draperies with cafe curtains
One traverse rod: decorative or conventional style; one or two-way draw.

One cafe rod
One pair or one panel of draperies depending on rod draw.

Cafe curtains
Tiebacks if desired
Cafe rings
Drapery hooks: purchase enough for cafe curtains unless using clip-on cafe rings

6. Cafe curtains
One or more cafe rods
Cafe curtains as required

Cafe rings
Drapery hooks unless using clip-on cafe rings

7. Curtains
Curtain rod of desired type
Curtains
Tiebacks if desired

8. Woven wood shade
One woven wood shade for inside or outside mounting. You will need to select a pattern, color and valance.

Woven woods are available as Roman, roller shades, etc. Your store can explain the various styles to you.

Check these off, too
1. Decorative rod styles. Select both style and finish.
Chateau
Sherwood
Atavio
Vintage: cafe rods are not available.
Mod-Rod: cafe rods are not available.
Traditional brass
Wood poles
2. Wood poles are not sold as sets. You will need to purchase the following parts and cut your pole to size.
Pole
Finials
Rings
Brackets
3. If you wish to tie back draperies, you may use any of the following items.
Metal chain tiebacks
Rope tiebacks
Self-tiebacks
Tieback holders: these decorative medallions may be used with any

tieback or alone, except at wide windows.
4. Several styles of drapery hooks are available.

Pin-on hooks should always be used for master slides and at returns. They are also used for draperies with "closed" bottom headings and for scalloped cafe curtains.

Slip-in hooks help pinch pleats stand erect. They are used for draperies with "open" bottom headings. These hooks come in several lengths which match various depths used for headings. There are also specific types for use with decorative and conventional traverse rods; these are not interchangeable.

Sew-on hooks
Easypleat hooks. These are for use with Easypleat drapery tape. They are not suitable for conventionally made draperies.
5. Window questions. It is not possible, here or anywhere, to completely answer all questions pertaining to window treatments. Interior designers, department stores, curtain and drapery shops, manufacturers, etc., are able to help with specific solutions. However, the amount of help depends on the information you give them about the problem.

It is best to have someone see the problem in your home. It is desirable to take a photo. And it is necessary to make a sketch with measurements.

Acknowledgments

138A (upper left). White and one hard-hitting blue turn this little room into a show-stopper! Notice how blue paint wipes out a radiator, too. Hung inside the window frame, both sets of shirred curtains are on spring pressure rods (page 122) — they need no brackets to install.

138B (upper right). Lavish is the only word for this, but the unique color scheme might live in much smaller quarters. Just balance it with lots of neutrals. The arches, obviously, are custom done. Use Kir-Flex rodding (page 123) for draperies.

138C (left). Three distinctly different patterns live in perfect harmony, united by their colors. Draw sheers will help to screen the sun and keep those colors bright. A lambrequin frames the window wall. Use a conventional traverse rod (pages 120, 121) for sheers.

Kirsch Company gratefully acknowledges the assistance and cooperation of the outstanding interior designers, photographers and other sources whose exceptional work is shown in this book. You'll find their names below.

Photography
James Brett
Robert Cleveland
Harold Davis
Max Eckert
Foto Graphics, Inc.
Freelance Photographers
Grignon Studios, Inc.
John Hartley
Hedrich-Blessing, Ltd.
Yuichi Idaka
Rich LaMar
Leland Lee
Paulus Leeser
Vincent Lisanti
Modernage, Inc.
Kent Oppenheimer
Richard Shirk
Everette Short
Vogue-Wright Studio

Other Photographs
Bride's Magazine
Collins and Aikman
Family Circle Magazine
Formica Corporation
Good Housekeeping Magazine
House & Garden Magazine
House Beautiful Magazine
Imperial Wall Coverings
Monsanto, Inc.
National Homes, Inc.
Vanguard Studios
Wallcovering Industry Bureau
Window Shade Manufacturers Assn.
Woman's Day Magazine

Designers
Harvey Ackerman
Kalef Alaton
Stanley Avelis
Elamay Barber
William Benner
Dorothy Baker Billings
Roger Billingsley
Blietz-Valenti
Sharon Carvell
Lou Cataffo
Lillian Chain
Jeanette Coppes
Abbey Darer
The Decorative Manner
Carole Eichen
Knowlton Fernald, Jr.
Virginia Frankel
Shirley Freemond
Gallerie, Ltd.
Pauline Gauthier
Andrew Gerhard
Charles Gibelterra
Harry Gladstone
Glenn Don Interiors
Ann M. Gray
Greta Grossman
Joyce Grossman Interiors
Guy-Hayden Associates
Habitational Designs
Tom Hadley
Marilynn Hansen
Gaylord Hauser
Ann Heller
Eleanor Hemstreet
Richard Himmel
Tom Irwin
Barbara Jewel
Steve Johnson
Gary Jon
Adele Keyes
Joanne Knaus
Joy Koch
Bill Lane
Roberta Lieberman
Bertie Litvin
Ruth Lynford
Shirley Lynn
Elizabeth MacDonald
Evelyn McCabe
Patrick Maas
Giorgio Marabito
Shirley Marks
Mattraw-Vickman Interiors
John Mauer
Mark Nelson
John A. Perkins
Pam Petit
J. Davis Polk
Janet Polizzi
Alan Portnoy
Tom Quaggin
Adelaide Radcliffe
Frances Ralston
Jacqueline Reaume
Shirley Regendahl
Claire Robinson
Phyllis Cole Rowen
Nadine Russell
Rita St. Clair
Saddleback Interiors
Ethel Samuels
Marcus Saxer
Florence Scanlin
Phyllis Serota
Morley Smith
Ronald Sorce
Pat Stafford
Karl Steinhauser
Donna Summers
Ruth Tay
George van Geldren
Tom Williams

Technical
Graphics Design, Schumaker Designers
Typography, Advertising Typographers, Inc.
Color Lithography, Precision Litho Plate, Inc.
Printing, Lehigh/Cadillac Printing, Inc.
Photo Stylist, Jessie Walker

"Windows Beautiful," Volume VI, is a publication of Kirsch Company, Sturgis, Michigan 49091. Questions regarding material in this book should be directed to that address. While we will do our best to supply information, it must be recognized that the vast majority of photos which appear here are of actual homes, and we respect the owners' right to privacy. Therefore, sources of furnishings and fabrics are frequently unavailable. Staff: Director, John J. Lichty; Editor, Roseann Fairchild; Production, Ronald E. Besser.

Index

IBC (right). There are ways to make more of a window than it is. For instance, this outward swinging casement is dressed as if it were an arch. Kir-Flex rodding (page 123) could form the gentle curve. Curtains are custom-made to fit the simulated arch.